GLENSHEE

Glen of the Fairies

GLENSHEE GLEN OF THE FAIRIES

500 Years of Life and Legend in a Highland Glen

ANTONY MACKENZIE SMITH

Watercolours by Philip Snow

TUCKWELL PRESS

First published in Great Britain in 2000 by
Tuckwell Press
The Mill House
Phantassie
East Linton
East Lothian, EH40 3DG
Scotland

1 86232 116 7

The publishers gratefully acknowledge the support
of the Scotland Inheritance Fund

British Library Cataloguing in Publication Data
A catalogue record for this book is available
on request from the British Library

Typeset and originated by Carnegie Publishing, Lancaster
Printed and bound by Book Print, Barcelona

Contents

Finegand Lodge, 1871

David   Sanderson   W. Shaw   A. Kirke Smith W. Smith A. M. Smith   Colin M. Smith

          Mrs Shaw   Sam   C. Shaw   Sandy McDonald

             Peter Shaw   Bang & Crack

Introduction

Since Man first appeared on this earth, he has been aware of special places – mountains, islands, rivers, groves of trees – Olympus, Delphi, Ganges. The list is endless and to it I would add Glenshee, or as it is in the Gaelic, *Gleann Shith*, the Glen of the Fairies. It has never had any other name, and until the old tongue died out the inhabitants were known as *Sithichean a' Ghlinnshith* or 'Elves of Glenshee'.

A cynical man who shall be nameless wrote that to describe a place as 'magical' was just to throw a worn ha'penny on the counter.

I do not agree.

Jean-Paul Sartre once said that the strongest argument for the existence of God was Man's need of him, and I believe the same applies to magic in whatever form we choose to find it.

It is not just fairies or kelpies, or even Italian swordsmen in league with the Powers of Darkness. It is not feats of superhuman strength or witches who turn themselves into vipers. Indeed, it is all these things, but it is also the impossible beauty of the Glen when seen from the top of the Brandywell at sunrise on a June morning. It is the spontaneous kindness of neighbours who help each other without being asked. It is the fearless love of the old widow who leaves her door open and a candle in the window just in case somebody, *anybody*, needs shelter for the night. It is the sympathy and understanding of the bank manager who will help a young farmer in trouble, and it is the simple humour of men who can laugh and joke and make light of hard work.

Long ago, my father told me the story of the man who discovered the difference between Hell and Heaven.

He once saw a long table laden with quantities of delicious food. Round it sat a company of people, each one holding a long spoon, so long in fact that none could feed himself. They were hungry, angry, frustrated, and curses and hatred were in the air.

He then saw another table, again laden with quantities of delicious food. Round it as before sat a company of people, each one holding a long spoon, but here there was contentment, happiness, love and laughter. Each person was feeding his neighbour.

I don't know where the first table is – probably in the boardroom of some huge corporation – but I believe the second table is in Glenshee and the assembled company are the *Sithichean* themselves.

If you don't believe in magic you may not be invited to the feast, but I think that when you have read my stories you will agree with me that there are still some fairies in the Glen.

1 *Childhood Memories*

There is nowhere in the world quite like my Glen. It is wild, romantic, unbelievably beautiful, and it is steeped in history and legend.

My family have lived there for five hundred years, and I have known it all my life. I have a thousand memories, but the earliest are of the river – the scent of the herbs along the water's edge and the plaintive but sweetly musical call of the sandpiper in the summer. I remember very clearly too that the sun shone every day, as it is obliged to do when one is five years old.

Fishing was a passion, and long before I could wield a rod I caught minnows in the river. This was tremendously exciting and required a special trap which had been made for me by a very old and kind river keeper called Hepplethwaite (*Mister* Hepplethwaite to us small boys) who had used a similar one when he was a boy. This quiet and charming man lived in Dunkeld in the winter, but in the summer he pitched a big square tent on a grassy lawn by the Loch of the Lowes, and here my brother and I would visit him in the evenings and he would tell us stories and make us minnow traps. I remember so well the smell of his pipe and his slow quiet voice, but above all I remember how wonderfully peaceful it was in that tent on the shore of the loch.

To make a minnow trap it was necessary to find a clear wine bottle with an inverted base. The apex of the base was then knocked out with a hammer and punch – an operation requiring both confidence and skill. Every time I tried it the bottle broke, but Mister Hepplethwaite seemed to find no difficulty. Three or four small pieces of red flannel were then tied at intervals along a piece of string which was lowered into the bottle and secured at the neck. A small piece of gauze or muslin was tied over the neck and the trap was complete. A shoal of minnows then had to be found by paddling slowly along in the clear, shallow

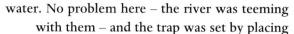

water. No problem here – the river was teeming with them – and the trap was set by placing the bottle with the neck facing upstream. Immediately, the current flowing through the bottle agitated the string and the pieces of red flannel began to move in a strange undulating motion.

The minnows were fascinated. They had never seen anything like this before and simply had to have a closer look. Most just stared through the sides of the bottle, but soon one found that he could see better by looking through the hole in the bottom. Curiosity overcame him and in he swam, soon to be followed by another, and another, till

> Thick and fast they came at last
> And more and more and more.

The excitement of watching this was unbearable, and all that limited the size of

The author as a boy, fishing in Glenshee

the catch and the population of our aquarium at home was the antics of the young minnow fishers jumping up and down in the water and frightening other victims away. It was enough to turn any five-year-old landlubber into a fisherman.

Next summer, one of my dreams came true. My godfather (one of many uncles) gave me a real split-cane trout rod. It was very light and, using both hands, I could just make a reasonable cast with it. Down to the river I hurried – I remember the exact spot at the end of a wall – and with beating heart cast my fly into the current. It was a glorious sunny day in the middle of May and my chief concern was that the only fly I possessed was a March Brown. However, I hoped the trout would not notice the discrepancy. One at least did not and there was a tug on my line. With a shout of joy I jerked the rod into the air and the little fellow came flying out of the water and landed at my feet. Not a technique, perhaps, for the serious salmon fisherman, but effective enough for a very small boy and a very small trout. Half an hour later, another, slightly smaller than the first, followed and I returned to the house with my catch. All that afternoon I basked in the admiration of those around me and my pleasure was all the more acute because my older brother had caught nothing. Obviously he had not been using a March Brown.

However, I remember a feeling of disappointment next morning when the two little fishes appeared on the breakfast table. Were they really as small as that? Yesterday they had seemed so much bigger and fatter. My feelings must have shown clearly, but my pride was saved by my mother explaining how much weight a fish would lose in the cooking. Darling Mother, she always made everything right for everyone.

A few years later, I think at the age of ten, I was allowed for the first time to go beating.

How important I felt! This was real man's work, and I looked forward eagerly to taking my place in the line.

A shooting day at Finegand was a great occasion, and early in the morning the various parties began to assemble in front of the house.

Uncle Billy and Charlie Lamond were the first to appear. They looked at the sky and discussed the direction of the wind – very important this, as a west or south wind would mean placing the guns in the lower butts, while a north or east wind would push the grouse higher up over the top butts.

Gradually other figures began to appear – keepers and ghillies in tweed suits and 'twa snooters'* and a large motley army of beaters – shepherds, farm boys,

---

* *deerstalkers or two-nosed bonnets.*

Billy shooting, 1935

the postman, the roadman, anyone old or young who could walk eight miles through the heather on a hot August day.

Two horses with huge wicker panniers stood quietly by ready to take up the lunch and bring down the grouse. Everybody had a job and knew exactly what it was. Uncle Billy was in charge of the guns, four family and four guests, and Charlie Lamond of the beaters. Johnny and Jimmie each had a horse and Aunt Mabel, a genius in such matters, arranged the lunch.

At nine o'clock, the beaters left in a fleet of cars, and I can still see my uncle's huge open Daimler driving off with his surly Yorkshire chauffeur and ten or twelve passengers, inside on the seats, outside on the running board, clinging to the luggage grid like passengers on a train in India. At nine thirty, they lined out on the northern march and the guns made their way to the butts. At ten o'clock, two shots were fired to start the beaters and then came the tense wait for the birds.

The butts were built on the reverse side of a small ridge so that the grouse could not be seen till they were about seventy yards away. Then they burst into view like small dark bullets, and in four seconds they were over the guns and away. A good shot, using two guns and a loader, might shoot two in front and two behind, but to do this perfect co-ordination and lightning reactions were necessary. It was Charlie Lamond's job to control the speed of the beaters so that the birds did not all go forward at once.

After the drive came the pick-up, and then another long wait while the beaters prepared for the next drive. After this came lunch and the guns were joined by the ladies and children too young to go beating. There was intense rivalry among the ladies of the county in this matter of shooting lunches, but my aunt was the undisputed Queen, and it was at one of these that I first graduated from ginger beer to the real thing.

There were two drives after lunch and for the first of these the ladies and children were allowed to join the guns in the butts – a privilege enjoyed, I suspect, more by the former than the latter. Silence and stillness, not easy for excited children, were imposed, and after the drive those who had behaved well were allowed to join in the pick-up.

At the end of the day the beaters were paid their wages of 7s. 6d. (37.5p)* and the family went home to Finegand for a very special sort of tea.

After my eight miles through the heather I had a hunger that can hardly be described, and I used to stand beside Mrs Lamond in the kitchen as she baked her wonderful girdle scones – the best in Scotland. When they were ready, I carried them, piping hot, into the dining room. Covered with home-made butter and heather honey, they were an unforgettable experience.

Round the table on these occasions there was always among the company a group of noisy and exuberant children, and the potential of these, mixed with melting butter and heather honey, can be imagined; but Aunt Mabel had the answer. Suspended over the table, like a huge brown spider, was a sponge on a piece of elastic, and this simple device not only dealt with the inevitable spills on the table, but also served, at the end of the meal, to clean up the horribly sticky faces and fingers of those who had feasted so well.

Mabel Fitzwilliam was one of the most delightful women of her generation. Sister of the seventh earl, she was a confirmed and active socialist all her life, and at the same time a true aristocrat from the top of her beautiful head to the ends of her (I have no doubt) beautiful toes. She had an air of authority, humour and serene goodwill which made her loved by all.

She first came to Finegand as a young bride in the summer of 1897 and the next morning, full of youthful energy, she went out for a walk before breakfast. Thrilled by the early morning air and the dew on the ground, and thinking herself alone, she went runnng and skipping through the newly harvested cornfield, gathering up her skirts and jumping over the stooks in uninhibited gaiety.

Alas! She had been seen in the distance by Charlie Lamond who stormed out

---

* This was the normal wage for a day's beating could be improved upon by the lucky few who managed to beat for the Spanish Royal Family who, every summer, took a moor near Aberfeldy. Here it was normal for the beaters to be regularly peppered with shot by the erratic and excitable Royal party. However, His Majesty was a kind and gracious man and the compensation, at so many pesetas per pellet, was so generous that there was always a long waiting list for this exciting and slightly dangerous job. To my intense disappointment I was never allowed to volunteer.

Lady Mabel Fitzwilliam

into the field shouting, 'Come back! Come back, ye daft lassie! Ye'll knock ower a' the stooks!' Poor Charlie! Imagine his horror and embarrassment when his 'daft lassie' turned out to be the young Lady Mabel herself!

She conducted her correspondence every day in a large sprawling hand and at lightning speed, and as every letter was finished she stuck it down and sat on it. By the end of the morning she would be sitting on a pile of twenty or thirty letters, and woe betide any of them that dared to come unstuck!

At her funeral in Sheffield the church was packed and there were three hundred people outside in the churchyard. I arrived late and was one of them.

Charlie Lamond himself was also an excellent letter writer with a clear hand and a quaint, old-fashioned turn of phrase. During the winter, he kept my uncle in Yorkshire fully informed of all the important events at Finegand – the prices of sheep and cattle, the depth of the snow, how many slates had blown off the roof in the night and so on, and one spring of a chance in a million. The previous August, the laird had been out shooting on the moor and somehow, at lunch, had lost his false teeth. Search was in vain, and he had gone back to Yorkshire without them. Next April, Charlie was burning heather as he did every year when, to his amazement, there among the blackened stems, something twinkled in the pale spring sunshine. Yes! It was indeed the laird's teeth, blackened a little by the fire and perhaps a trifle melted, but still intact and serviceable.

AT SHEEP SALE. — Mr Charles Lamond, Finegand, Glenshee, provides an interesting character study at the sheep sale at Blairgowrie. Farmers and shepherds from the hills attended in force.

Charlie wrote at once and placed them on the mantelpiece where they sat and waited with a crooked grin. When the laird returned, he presented them with a proud flourish but was sadly disappointed when they were not immediately returned to his mouth. Billy, obviously unaware of this impending miracle, had, on his return to Yorkshire, purchased a fine new set.

As Charlie got older, Johnny and Jimmie did all the farm work and he just tended the sheep on the hill, which in summer meant sleeping quietly with his back against a stone. He was as fine an old Highlander as one could wish to meet, a superb farmer, a born shepherd, and all his life one of the stalwarts of the Glenshee Rifle Club.

Sadly, by the time I returned to the Glen he and his wife had died, and Johnny and Jimmie and Nan and Lizzie had moved down to Bridge of Cally.

2 *Return to the Glen*

It was a cool April day when I returned to live in the Glen, and as my car (a little green MG, absolutely immaculate although as Slipper might have said 'about the one age wit' meself') topped the Lair Brae at the bottom of the Glen, I stopped and got out and took deep breaths of the mountain air. We had always done this as children – it was a sort of ritual – and the air was just as I remembered it, unbelievably cool and pure with a faint but clear bouquet which changed with the seasons: larch and pine in the spring and the rich heavy scent of heather in the autumn.

There, across the river, was Dalnaglar Castle, tall, white, unmistakably Victorian and in perfect harmony with the dark green woods surrounding it. The little towers and turrets were reminiscent of Hans Anderson or Grimm, and I am sure the fairies had always loved it. A little further on I passed the Cockstone or Clach-na-Coileach, a huge boulder close to the road where we often used to lunch on shooting days. How it got this strange name is a story which I will tell you later. All the way up the Glen there were familiar sights. First, Tigh-na-Coile with its neat little garden tucked away in the woods. Here I could picture old Mrs M'Donald standing in the doorway in her bonnet and long black dress, as proud and dignified as the old Queen she had seen so many times in her coach, driving up to Balmoral. Then Polgorm, the old white farmhouse and barns of Finegand, the red roof of Cnoc Liath peeping over the birchwoods, and finally my destination, Corrydon Lodge.

Here I was to spend two uneasy months in an atmosphere which at first I could not explain. I had, of course, known the house all my life but had never lived in it, and now that I was doing so I felt uncomfortable. This feeling persisted but never changed, and I had been there about a week when one day I saw an

Mrs M'Donald

ancient figure approaching down the road. This was 'Old Grewar' who had been the roadman in Glenshee for as long as anyone could remember. His son Peter was notoriously fond of a dram and was the most skilful poacher for miles around, but the old man was, so he told me, both sober and honest. Old-fashioned, formal and polite, he was the only one left who spoke the Gaelic, and he knew the names of all the fields and streams and corries. But, more important for me, he knew all the old stories and legends of the Glen.

This morning, as he approached with his shovel on his shoulder, I greeted him and, as usual, he seemed willing, for the sake of good manners, to postpone his important work for as long as I wished. He was genuinely pleased to see me back in the Glen and asked with polite interest how I was getting on with the farm work, had it been a good lambing, and so on, and then, with a keen, searching look of his old blue eyes, how did I like living at Corrydon? I told him quite honestly that I did not like it at all. 'Nae wonder. I'm no' surprised at all, at all. It'll be yon auld man buried under the hoose.'

I knew nothing of this. No doubt my parents thought it better that I should not know, but I made no reply, waiting for the story. When it came it concerned the famous M'Comie Mor, laird of Finegand in the seventeenth century. It appeared that one day when M'Comie was away from home a big stout caird or travelling pedlar had called at Finegand and, finding no man there, had behaved very rudely to the ladies in the house. Whether this rudeness had taken the form of undue pressure to buy his wares or improper suggestions we will never know. However, what had taken place was reported to M'Comie on his return and he, furiously demanding which way the caird had gone, took two swords from their place on the wall and set off in pursuit. Coming up with the caird opposite Broughdearg, he gave the unfortunate man his choice of the swords and told him to defend himself. It was an unequal contest. M'Comie, as you will learn, was the finest swordsman of his day and the caird was soon despatched. He was buried where he fell, and remained undisturbed for two hundred and fifty years.

But then my great-uncle Alexander Mackenzie Smith – 'Uncle Mac' as he was known to all the family – decided to build himself a new house where he and all his many relations could spend the summer. The site he chose was Imir-a-Chaird, the Caird's Field. Local people who knew the story warned him not to build there, but Uncle Mac knew better, at least until the foundations were pre-pared, for then there lay exposed the skeleton of a man.

The workmen were dismayed and, having reverently removed the bones, asked what they should do. Now Uncle Mac, though his mother was a Mackenzie and a true Highlander, had a Yorkshire father whose practical nature he inherited. 'Put him back,' he said, 'He's been there a long time.' And so the caird was gently returned to his old resting place and the house was completed.

Nowadays, if you pass by of an evening you may still see, as several of my family have, the figure of a Highlander dressed in an old ragged plaid walking in the garden.

Some weeks after this conversation with Grewar, I had occasion to lunch with my friend Lady Owen, a lively old lady of eighty, very proud of her Mackenzie ancestry. I told her about the caird but was rather disappointed that she did not seem to be in the least surprised. Of course, I realise that finding a skeleton in one's garden in the Highlands may be less unusual than a similar discovery in, say, Wimbledon or Woking, but still I was slightly deflated by the calm way she capped my story. 'These things used to happen all the time in the Highlands,' she said. 'A few years ago, my gardener here at Merklands dug up a skeleton. I remember it was in perfect condition – except for a large hole in the top of its head.'

Fortunately, I was soon able to move to Finegand because it had been arranged that the grieve, the cattleman and the carter should retire that summer. They were all either side of eighty years old and McColl, the carter, a small man with a gnarled brown face and very twinkly eyes, was suffering from the effect of an old wound received in the Boer War. This had given him a pronounced limp, made worse by long hours and years of ploughing with one foot on the land and the other in the furrow.

This spring, the problem had been getting worse and he had been falling over from time to time as he ploughed. The only reason the work had been completed at all was because Wallace and Donald, the two Clydesdale horses, knew and loved the old man, and whenever he fell they stopped at once, looked round together and waited for him to get to his feet. As soon as he gathered up the reins, they plodded steadily on. They both understood exactly what to do, and it was a touching sight to see these two fine creatures taking such care of their master.

I was a lucky young man to be taught to plough by such an artist as old McColl.

The next job to be done was the singling of the turnips, agreed by all to be the most boring job on the farm. They had been sown before I arrived and, fresh from Agricultural College, I had suggested to the old grieve before he retired that perhaps this was rather an outdated crop, for was a turnip not, after all, ninety percent water? He silenced me with sixty-five years of practical experience. 'Aye, maybe, but ninety percent o' muckle powerful watter!'

I started the dreaded job with just two men to help me, my shepherd and a hired man. The field was only seven acres, but as I looked at the seemingly endless drills, it might as well have been seventy. We worked steadily on without much conversation, and in the middle of the morning I looked round and, to my surprise, there were three men behind me, not two. An hour later, there were five, not three. My helpers had come from over the river and seeing me, as they thought, behind with the work, had crossed the water and, without a word, had fallen in behind me. They came every day as soon as their own work was done, and by the end of the week my field was finished.

Such were my neighbours in Glenshee – Sandy Grant, Alec Duff and Charlie Stewart. Did I not just say that I was a lucky young man? And did I not say too that in the Glen of the Fairies there is still a little magic in the air?

Sandy's father, Dan Grant, had been an equally good neighbour in his day, but a strict man who expected the same exact standards from his neighbours as he did from his own family. In those days the river bank was not fenced on either side and a Finegand sheep would occasionally, in summer, find its way over onto Dan's land. (For some reason his sheep never crossed onto our land and I can only suppose that this was because he had forbidden them to do so). Our wayward animal would be immediately impounded and a messenger, usually one of the children, sent to Finegand to say that it was shut in Dan's barn awaiting collection by its owner. These messages invariably ended with the firm reminder, 'The boundary is the middle of the water!'

Clipping, on the other hand, (*clipping* not *shearing*: there were no machines in the Glen in those days) was, unlike hoeing the 'neeps', a happy social occasion where everyone joined in and the hard work was forgotten in the laughter, jokes and teasing that went on all day.

It started with the early morning gathering which I found the most exhilarating and enjoyable experience in all my life as a hill farmer. There are, of course, highs and lows in every farmer's life and sometimes, as you will hear, the lows can be devastating, but these summer mornings were unforgettable and made up for all the hardships of winter.

We set off at five o'clock and, as the sun rose and the mist smoked off the heather, the full, pure beauty of the Glen emerged. The wild creatures were now awake, and we could see the shy roe deer in their russet summer coats feeding along the top of the birchwoods with their tiny fawns beside them. The mountain hares too, who had been pure white all winter, had put on their summer clothes – smart brown and slate-grey suits of soft fur. The grouse and golden plover had finished nesting and watched anxiously over their broods as the circling dogs raced past them. It was a perfect world where evil just did not, *could not*, exist and I am truly sorry for those who have never known such a place. Since the days of Our Lord in Galilee, the shepherd has been a much-loved icon, and in truth he is one of the luckiest men on earth.

We arrived down at the fank at about seven o'clock and the sheep were left to cool and rest while we had breakfast. Then the real work started.

There would be two men catching, eight or ten clipping, two rolling the fleeces and one packing these into huge sacks or sheets. Speed was essential and, though the chaff and banter went on all day, so did the work. Mistakes occurred (specially among the inexperienced) and the occasional ewe would disappear with a tuft of unclipped wool sticking to her backside – gales of laughter and good natured sarcasm – but the spectacle most enjoyed was when a half-clipped ewe escaped and ran off, trailing her fleece behind her like a bride's dress.

As the day wore on, we began to tire. It was summer, and sweat became mixed with the sweet smell of lanoline on our clothes. Backs, old and young alike, began to ache and the jokes to fade.

Then, suddenly, as one more ewe, all unaware of her privileged position, leapt from the clipping green, we heard the triumphant cry we had all been waiting for, 'That's the one the cobbler killed his wife wi'!'

'What one's that, Jimmy?'

'The last!'

And so the sheep, now snowy white and delighted to be rid of their winter garment, went racing and jumping back to the hill and we all went in to the shepherd's house for a real Scotch high tea – sausages, bacon, black puddings, scones, jam, honey and quarts of strong, sweet tea. We ate like heroes, but I have never seen a fat shepherd.

One of the new ideas I tried was growing seed potatoes. The land was not all that good and the season was short but, at 1000 feet above sea level, the aphid which carried potato virus could not survive and so the crop was virus-free and very valuable.

Growing the potatoes was not very difficult, but the 'tatty picking' in the autumn was another matter altogether. A large gang was needed to gather the potatoes uncovered by the digger, and the only folk available were the tinkers from Blairgowrie, famous for their drunken, thieving ways if they didn't like you and for their loyalty, wit and charm if they did. I hoped they would like me, but I was by no means sure if they would. After my long absence from the Glen they might even have thought I was an Englishman. However, with a brave face I went down to their camp and asked for the senior member.

This turned out to be a handsome, red-haired woman of about forty, and she seemed willing to provide a gang – the berry picking was long past, the low ground tatties were all lifted and work was scarce. It was arranged that they would come for a week and, as I turned to go, a girl ran towards me. She was the woman's daughter, fifteen or sixteen years old, ragged, untidy and none too clean, but wildly, heart-stoppingly beautiful and with the naughtiest eyes I have ever seen. With a bar of soap and a hairbrush she could have conquered the world. She came right up to me and with a wicked smile said, 'Can I come too?'

She was irresistible and without a thought I said, 'Yes, yes, of course.'

'And if I come to Finegand for a week, what will my job be?'

I was saved by an angry shout from her mother.

'Come away, Jeannie, and mind your manners!'

When the gang arrived next day, I looked for Jeannie, not quite sure if I wanted to see her or not. I sensed trouble, the least of which would be the teasing of my neighbours; but there she was, as impudent as ever. Work went on well till the first tea break, but then the tractor refused to start. The gang reclined on the headland in the warm autumn sunshine, smoking, chatting and very much at ease. The tractor was an old one and started with a handle, but it always *did* start. Why not now? My shepherd, Jim Mann, was an expert motor mechanic, but he too was baffled and it was another half-hour before we found the cause. By some absolutely miraculous chance, a small potato had found its way into the exhaust pipe. It was removed and work went on till dinner time at noon. The gang had all brought their 'piece' and bottles of lemonade and milk, and at half past twelve we started again. My job was tractor driver, and half way down the first drill my eye caught sight of a glint in the earth just in front of the tyre. I got down and found a milk bottle with a broken jagged top just sticking out of the ground. A burst tyre would have ended the day and I lost my temper. I told them they were a lazy, good-for-nothing bunch of scoundrels and they could b ..... well get back in their rusty old cars and go home.

But work was scarce, and though an occasional extra break was one thing, to be sent home without pay was quite another. They all assured me that 'Whatever monkey was playing tricks on me wouldnae dae it again.' Of course I knew, we all did, who the monkey was. She apologised and told me I was the handsomest man she had ever seen (a lie, of course, but it worked). I forgave her and told her she was the wickedest and most beautiful girl in the world, and on that happy understanding we worked together for the rest of the week. I never saw her again, but I feel sure she bought a hairbrush and married a prince.

My potatoes, clean, healthy and virus-free, were bought by a merchant with a big export business and by December were all on their way to exotic, far away countries – Egypt, Israel and Tenerife.

As the icy fingers of winter tightened their grip on the Glen, and the snow wreaths gathered round my door, how often did I think of them, snug and happy in the soft, warm earth on the banks of the Nile!

The merchant, whose name was W....., became a good friend of mine. He was a large, genial man with a great sense of humour, and was the best-liked and (until he went bankrupt) the most successful potato merchant in the east of Scotland.

I don't remember the make of his car, but the number was POT 80.

The following February, disaster struck in the form of a ferocious storm which arrived with the sudden force of a train coming out of a tunnel. In the teeth of a howling wind and driving snow, Jim Mann tried desperately to get the sheep down off the hill to the comparative safety of the fields by the river. He managed this on all the ground except for about a hundred ewes in Corrydon, and in the afternoon we set off together to find these. It was still snowing hard, the wind was stronger than ever and the drifts were waist deep as we struggled up the path to the corrie, but in the end we found about forty of them. There was no way that they could get down through the drifts, so Jim and I had to make a path for them. This we did by forcing our way through the snow and beating it down with our feet and arms. The little path we made like this was only a few feet wide and the drifting snow filled it in almost as fast as we made it, but Jim's old dog, Queen, drove the ewes on behind us in single file as if she knew their lives depended on her efforts. By dark, we had our little flock down off the hill, but a count next day showed that there were fifty-seven missing.

However, there is always hope when sheep are buried. We both knew they can survive for days under the snow. It melts around them, leaving a frozen roof over their heads, and they live in a sort of air pocket, drinking from the snow and scraping underfoot for heather and grass.

Morning after morning Jim and I forced our way back up the corrie, carrying with us long thin hazel poles with which we poked and prodded all the drifts in the hope of feeling some movement. Evening after evening we returned, utterly exhausted, having found nothing.

Eventually, we both realised it was hopeless, and I got into the Landrover and drove slowly down the Glen to see my bank manager. I feared that my farming career was over almost before it had begun, and this was not an interview I was looking forward to. As I walked into his office the first thing that struck me was how warm it was. (At Finegand I had no electricity and no heating except the Rayburn in the kitchen.) A wave of resentment came over me and I thought, why should this plump little man sit here in such comfort while Jim and I are up to our armpits in the snow?

Then I looked again at the plump little man and my resentment vanished. The expression on his face was a mixture of kindness, sympathy and understanding.

'Yes, indeed,' he said. 'It was a terrible storm. How many have you lost?'

'Fifty-seven,' I said. 'A disaster at any time, but this is my first winter!'

'How long have your family been in the Glen?' he said.

'Nearly five hundred years,' I answered.

'And do you think this is the first such storm in five hundred years?'

'Well, no, I'm sure it's not.'

'Your family have been there for five hundred years and I will personally see that you are there next year – and the year after.'

God bless him! He was just the manager of a small bank in Blairgowrie, but I felt he should have been Governor of the Bank of England. Surely some of the magic of the Glen had followed me down the road. Two years later the farm was making record profits, and as I write today the family are more firmly established there than ever before.

A couple of weeks after I moved into Finegand, I made one of my worst mistakes. I had to go to a sale in Perth and I set off early, locking the front door behind me as I left. It was evening when I returned and my letters were in the porch.

Next morning, the postman, Bob Stewart, came as usual. We always had a friendly chat when he brought the letters, but this morning he looked unusually serious.

'Ye were awa' yesterday.'

'Yes, Bob, I went to the sale in Perth.'

'I ken that fine, and ye lockit your door.'

I admitted that I had done so, and Bob politely explained his problem. Finegand had one of only three telephones in the Glen, and since its installation three years before, Bob, who was a keen racing man, had been in the habit of placing his bets in this way. The day before, it transpired, he had had a dead cert for the second race at Ayr, and had come down to Finegand, full of confidence, to place his bet with the bookmaker in Blairgowrie. He was dismayed to find the door 'lockit', and of course I need not tell you that the horse won at ridiculous odds.

I apologised abjectly and never, ever, 'lockit' my door again. In Glenshee it was an unheard-of thing to do. From time immemorial it had been a custom in the Highlands to keep an open door and a candle in the window to guide the weary traveller to a safe haven. I had forgotten much.

Unfortunately, this tradition has now completely died out. As recently as the winter of 1998, a young girl walking home from a party near Perth became lost in a snowstorm. She perished from the cold in the corner of a field, but was less than two hundred yards from a farmhouse. If only there had been a candle in the window!

Two years later, at the beginning of March, I went ski-ing in Austria. While I was away, one of my friends, Peter Carmichael, took his wife and children up to the new chairlift on the Cairnwell. While they were ski-ing the wind rose and snow began to fall. Peter decided they should set off for home in case the road became blocked. As they motored down the Glen, the drifts got deeper and deeper, and soon it became evident that they would never get home that night. The danger was that if they got stuck they would not be able to leave the car because the snow was too deep for the children. It was, in fact, a pretty grim situation, but Peter said, 'Never mind, children, we'll just go and stay with Tony at Finegand.'

They managed – just – to reach the house, but to their dismay it was dark and empty. Their hearts sank, but Peter got out of the car and tried the door. Dismay turned to joy and relief – it was unlocked! They all went in and soon found candles and paraffin lamps and made themselves at home. Because in those days the big blower snowploughs were still a thing of the distant future, it was quite common for the road to be blocked for anything up to a week, and all the houses in the Glen were well stocked with food and fuel. Peter soon had the Rayburn lit and supper on the table, and there they stayed, warm and comfortable, for four days, while the big plough slowly punched its way up the Glen to their rescue.

Soon after my return from Austria, I received an invitation to dine with Peter and his family. By then my little MG had been replaced by a Triumph TR, a small two-seater with a large boot, and as I drove home after dinner I became concerned by the behaviour of the car. The nose semed light and it weaved a little from side to side. However, I put this strange sensation down to my last glass of brandy and drove with exaggerated care.

It was not for several days that I had occasion to open the boot, and when I did so all became clear. It was stuffed completely full with drink – whisky, gin, champagne, wine, everything that a serious drinking man could wish for. It must have been packed during dinner and the weight of it had almost lifted the front wheels off the road. What generosity! It would have taken Uncle Mac himself a year to get through it.

Every summer, my uncle came up from Yorkshire to stay with me. He was my father's eldest brother and had been laird for fifty years. A mere eighty-four years old, he could still carry a gun to the highest point of the hill in the morning and come home again in the afternoon with a bag of grouse on his back. He loved the Glen as much as I did, and his knowledge of it and the Mackenzies was quite remarkable for a man who relied almost entirely on his memory. We talked for hours, or rather he talked and I listened, and all the time he kept saying, 'Write it down, Tony, write it down before you forget.' I'm glad to say that I took his advice and did so, and to add to my store of knowledge he gave me books and portraits and old photographs which he had collected over the

'Billy' – Col. William Mackenzie Smith, DSO, TD, LLD

years. Unfortunately, some of these have been burnt, but others remain and are treasured possessions.

But it was not just the laird who came to stay. All through the summer, the house seemed to be full of friends and relations. They had to amuse themselves during the week because I was busy with the farm work, but on Sundays we all went to the Kirk at the head of the Glen where we were subjected to interminable sermons from the learned old minister from Cray – a classical scholar who studied the Scriptures as readily in ancient Greek as he did in English. This delightful little church was completed in 1822 to replace the original rude and primitive building known as the Chapel of Ease, where monthly services had been held by the minister from Kirkmichael. All vestiges of this old chapel have long since disappeared, but we have a fascinating description of it from one of Scotland's greatest poets, the Ettrick Shepherd, who wrote in 1829:

> About thirty years ago, I first visited the Spital of Glenshee, and at that time I had never seen a greater curiosity than the place of worship there. It is a Chapel of Ease belonging to a parish called Kirkmichael, is built of stone and lime, and the roof is flagged with slate. The door was locked, but both the windows were wide open, without either glass or frame, so that one stepped as easily in at the windows as at the door. There were no seats, but here and there a big stone was placed, and as things of great luxury, there were two or three sticks laid from one of these to another. The floor was literally paved with human bones, and I saw that the dogs had gnawed the ends of many of them by way of amusing themselves in the time of worship. When the service was over, the minister gathered the collection for the poor on the green, in the crown of his hat, and neither men nor women thought of dispersing, but stood in clubs about the Chapel, conversing, some of them for upwards of an hour. I have seen many people who appeared to pay more attention to the service, but I never saw any who appeared to enjoy the crack after the sermon so much.

He was not aware, when he wrote this, that the dreadful old building he described had been replaced, nor did he know the strange reason that the new church had been built on the site of the old one. This was explained to me by the minister one Sunday afternoon after the service. Apparently, when the building of the new church was being discussed, there had been different opinions as to where it should be sited, but eventually, after much discussion by the appropriate committee, it was decided that Runavey, being more central to the Glen, was the best place, and work started. However, the fairies who, as you know, have always taken a keen interest in the affairs of the Glen, did not approve

Glenshee Church and the Auld Brig, 1913

of the change of location, and when the builders started work they removed each night the stones which had been put in place by day. This continued night after night, until the committee at last decided that it was useless to oppose the wishes of the Little People, and the new church was built on the site of the old one.

Although it is evident from the above that the early ministers of Kirkmichael may have neglected the fabric of some of their outlying chapels, we must not assume that they were equally lax in caring for the ultimate salvation of their parishioners. Human frailty, then as now, was not uncommon and there were inevitable falls from Grace among his flock, but it was the duty of the minister to see that these soul-endangering lapses did not recur. Punishment and repentance were necessary as we can see from this extract from the records of the kirk-session of Kirkmichael:

March 2, 1651

Ilk day Johne M'Intoishe of ffanneyzeand, Thomas Keill, and Alexr. M'Intoishe in Derrow, his tennants, maid public satisfaction in sackcloth, and gave [due] evidences of yr. repentances for deceiving the minister be causing him baptize ane chyld gottin in fornication, under the notione of a lawll. chyld.

My uncle David could remember when the minister at the Spital Kirk would pray for protection from 'witches and warlocks and things that go bump in the night'. In those days the men would walk as much as ten miles over the hills to attend the services, and their dogs sat in the pews with them. My uncle hoped the Elders never found themselves in the position of the authorities of St Margaret's, Westminster who, in the late 1600s, entered in their accounts: 'Paid for salt to kill the fleas in the churchwarden's pew, sixpence'.

He also recalls that 'In 1855 a certain Mr ... combined the offices of minister and apothecary in the Glen. Wherever he went he was accompanied by a big dog. One of my father's brothers and a farm hand at Finegand were suffering from sore throats. Mr ... was summoned to attend them. He produced an instrument of curved whalebone with a small sponge attached to it, which he covered with caustic; he then proceeded to work the sponge up and down my uncle's throat as though cleaning a gun barrel. Having finished with his first victim he wiped the sponge on the dog's back and operated on the farm labourer.'

The unfortunate relative subjected to this rough and ready treatment was Uncle Mac, a large and extravert character who enjoyed all that life had to offer – good sport, good wine and good company. He lived happily at Corrydon for thirty years and never gave a thought to the poor caird under the dining-room floor. His stout, kilted figure was a well-known landmark on the road to Braemar for, when not shooting or fishing, he would have a table set up on the side of the road outside his front door. On this was a liberal supply of champagne, and no traveller was allowed to pass by without joining him for a glass – or two.

The long, sloping hill on the south march of Finegand is known as the Brandywell, and got its name in this way. One day Uncle Mac was out shooting with a party, and when lunchtime came they all sat down round a small well, or spring, in the heather. When lunch was over, Uncle Mac turned to his keeper, Sandy M'Donald, and said, 'Come now, join us in a glass of brandy'. But Sandy, though by no means teetotal, on this occasion declined. Instead, he took the proffered glass and tipped the contents into the well, saying as he did so, 'I'll nae tak' your drink, but there'll be brandy and water here for ever'.

Remembering this, I have often drunk from the little well when shooting or gathering sheep, but I confess that it is only in my imagination that I taste Uncle Mac's brandy.

He was the eldest of Mary Anne Mackenzie's ten sons. He died in 1906, and the estate passed into the safe and capable hands of his nephew Billy, who was laird for fifty years. It was perhaps fortunate for all of us that the succession missed out Uncle Mac's next brother, Thomas, for he was a wild and reckless young man who could easily have lost it. Like all the family, he was a superb horseman, and one day he decided that perhaps America might offer a more exciting life than England. He set off and soon found himself working as a cowboy on a ranch in Texas. It was 1870 when the West was at its wildest, and Thomas was as wild as any of it. One night, after a bunkhouse party, he bet his comrades that he could swim the Rio Grande on his horse. By chance I happen to know the Rio Grande – it is a fast and dangerous river which has claimed the lives of many a 'wetback' trying to swim from Mexico to America. Some weeks later, my grandfather received a letter from the owner of the ranch saying how sorry he was that Thomas had disappeared that night and no trace of him had ever been found. The letter ended with a short postscript which probably meant as much to the rancher who wrote it as to the Master of Foxhounds who received it: 'The horse was recovered'.

Sandy M'Donald

3 The Mackenzies

It is generally known that the natural home of the Mackenzies is Kintail in the north-west of Scotland, and how a branch of this illustrious clan came to be established in Braemar and Glenshee is a tale of love, courage, treachery and ultimate reward. It has been put together by Alexander Mackenzie, the foremost historian of the clan, and I can do no better than quote from his most comprehensive work. If the language appears somewhat quaint, it is because the story is derived almost entirely from sixteenth- and seventeenth-century manuscripts:

> When, in 1488, King James IV succeeded to the throne of Scotland, he determined to attach to his interest the principal chiefs in the Highlands. To overawe and subdue the petty princes who affected independence, to carry into their territories, hitherto too exclusively governed by their own capricious or tyrannical institutions, the same system of a severe but regular and rapid administration of civil and criminal justice which had been established in his Lowland dominions, was the laudable object of the king; and for this purpose he succeeded, with that energy and activity which remarkably distinguished him, in opening up an intercourse with many of the leading men in the northern counties. With the Captain of the Clan Chattan, Duncan MacIntosh, with Ewan the son of Alan, Captain of the Clan Cameron, with the Lairds of Mackenzie and Grant; and the Earl of Huntly, a baron of the most extensive power in these northern districts, he appears to have been in habits of constant and regular communication – rewarding them by presents, in the shape of money or grants of land, and securing their services in reducing to obedience such of their fellow chieftains as proved contumacious or actually rose in rebellion.

MACKENZIE

R. R. McIan. pinxit.   Russell, Lith.

BUCHANAN

To carry out this plan he determined to take pledges for their good behaviour from some of the most powerful clans, and at the same time educate the younger lairds into a more civilized manner of governing their people. Among others, he took a special interest in Kenneth Og and Farquhar Macintosh, the young lairds of Mackenzie and MacIntosh who were cousins, their mothers being sisters, daughters of John, last Lord of the Isles. They were both powerful, the leaders of great clans and young men of great spirit and reckless habits. They were accordingly apprehended in 1495 and sent to Edinburgh. According to Sir George Mackenzie's MS history of the clan, 'The king, having made a progress to the north, was advised to secure these two gentlemen as hostages for securing the peace of the Highlands, and accordingly they were apprehended at Inverness and sent prisoners to Edinburgh in the year 1495, where they remained two years'.

They were kept in custody in the castle until, a favourable opportunity occuring in 1497, they escaped over the ramparts by the aid of ropes secretly conveyed to them by some of their friends. This was the more easily managed as they had liberty granted to them to roam over the whole bounds of the castle within the outer walls; and the young chieftains, getting tired of restraint and ashamed to be idle while they considered themselves to be fit actors for the stage of their Highland domains, resolved to attempt an escape by dropping over the walls, when Kenneth injured his leg so as to incapacitate him from rapid progress; but MacIntosh manfully resolved to risk capture himself rather than leave his fellow fugitive behind him in such circumstances. The result of this accident, however, was that after three days journey they were only able to reach the Torwood where, suspecting no danger, they put up for the night in a private house.

The Laird of Buchanan, who was at the time an outlaw for a murder he had committed, happened to be in the neighbourhood and, meeting the Highlanders, entertained them with a show of kindness, by which means he induced them to divulge their names and quality. A proclamation had recently been issued promising remission to any outlaw who would bring in another similarly circumstanced, and Buchanan resolved to procure his own freedom at the expense of his fellow fugitives, for he knew well that such they were, previously knowing them as His Majesty's pledges for their repective clans.

In the most deceitful manner, he watched until they had retired to rest, when he surrounded the house with a band of his followers and charged them to surrender. This they declined, and Mackenzie, being of a violent temper and possessed of more courage than prudence, rushed out with a drawn sword 'refusing delivery and endeavouring to escape', whereupon he was shot with an arrow by one of Buchanan's men. His head was severed from his body and forwarded to the king in Edinburgh; while young MacIntosh, who made no further resistance, was secured and sent a prisoner to the king. Buchanan's outlawry was remitted and MacIntosh was confined in Dunbar, where he remained until after the death of James IV at the Battle of Flodden Field.

Buchanan's base conduct was universally execrated, while the fate of young Mackenzie was lamented throughout the whole Highlands, having been accused of no other crime than the natural forwardness of youth, and having escaped from his confinement in Edinburgh Castle.

It is admitted on all hands that Kenneth Og was killed in 1497 and he must therefore, his father having died in 1491, have ruled as one of the Barons of Kintail, though there is no record of his having been formally served heir. He was not married, but left two sons – one, known as Rory Beag, by the daughter of the Baron of Moniack, and the other by the daughter of a Gentleman in Cromar, of whom are descended the Sliochd Thomais in Cromar and Glenshee, the principal families of which are those of Dalmore and Renoway (Runavey).

Another ancient MS states, 'In his going to Inverness, as I have said, to meet the King, he (Mackenzie) was the night before his coming there in the Baron of Moniack's house, whose daughter he got with child, who was called Rory Begg. Of this Rory descended the parson of Slate; and on the same journey, going along with the king to Edinburgh, he got a son with a gentleman's daughter and called him Thomas Mackenzy, of whom descended the Mackenzies in Braemar called *Slyghk Homash Vic Choinnich*, that is to say Thomas Mackenzie's succession.

Such is the account given by Alexander Mackenzie, and a similar story has been handed down in my own family for hundreds of years, with the graceful addition that King James, regretting the untimely fate of the young chief whose father had been his friend, enquired if he had left no heirs, and bestowed the Dalmore estate upon his son.

But that is not the end of the story of Kenneth Og. Tradition has preserved a curious anecdote connected with the Mackenzies whose young chief, John of Kintail, was taken prisoner at Flodden. The foster-brother of Kenneth Og was a man of the district of Kinlochewe named Donald Dubh MacGillecrist vic Gilleroch, who, with the rest of the clan, was at Flodden with his chief. In the retreat of the Scottish army, this Donald Dubh heard someone near him exclaiming, 'Alas, Laird, thou hast fallen'. On enquiry, he was told that this was the Laird of Buchanan, who had sunk from his wounds or exhaustion. The faithful Highlander, eager to avenge the death of his chief and foster-brother, drew his sword and saying, 'If he has not fallen, he shall fall,' made straight for Buchanan whom he killed on the spot.

And so the infant Thomas M'Kenzie became laird of Dalmore in 1497. Unfortunately, we do not know whom he eventually married, but we do know that he had a son Kenneth who, as a young man, appears to have been in the service of Invercauld. Tradition has it that he was a handsome youth, and why should he not have been, descended from the Barons of Kintail and the Lords of the Isles?

He must have been born, I suppose, about the year 1520, for he was married to the daughter of Finlay Mor before that great laird fell, bearing the Royal Standard, at the battle of Pinkie. Here is the story of his marriage:

> Finlay's daughter, called, after her mother, Beatrix, when in the flower of her youth, was considered the finest damsel on Dee. It is needless therefore to say that many young men 'cam' seekin' her to woo'. Her father would have been glad to see her choose a partner suitable to her rank. Unfortunately for this consummation devoutly to be desired, a fine young lad, Kenneth M'Kenzie, one of his shepherds, found more favour in Miss Farquharson's eyes than the bravest gallants in Mar. When Finlay got into the secret, he pested and stormed and said some very ugly Gaelic words. But remembering the standing in days of yore of a certain Fearchar Cam nan Gad, and the later doings of a certain Donald M'Fearchar, he consoled himself with that most philosophic axiom 'It's weel it's nae waur' and had the couple married.
>
> 'Now, my lad,' quoth Finlay, 'if there's any bit of land you would like to live on more than another, just say the word, and welcome to it.' 'If that be the case,' quoth the knowing Kenneth, 'we will go and build our house *air an Dail Mhor ghorm ud fada shuas* (on that big green haugh far west) where we can get a bite for the beasties.' So the young couple pitched their tent there, and begat sons and daughters, and waxed great and mighty.

In fact, it was not really surprising that Invercauld gave his blessing to the young couple, for their story was strangely similar to that of his own father. Let me tell you how the Farquharsons came to Braemar:

> One day a poor man, a basket maker named Fearchar Shaw or Fearchar

Linn of Dee

Cam nan Gad, One eyed
Fearchar of the Wands
as he was known,
came down from
Speyside into Brae-
mar. He worked
hard and long and earned a scanty living until the sad day came when,
cutting withies by the Linn o' Dee, he tumbled into the river and disappeared. His frantic wife searched all day, but there was no sign of Fearchar,
and when night came she sat down, weeping and exhausted, by Tober
Moire, the Well of St Mary of Inverey. Here she took out her beads and,
telling them over and over, she begged the Blessed Virgin to intercede with
her Son to reveal the body of Fearchar Cam. Her devotion was rewarded,
for when morning came and she returned to the waterside, there, on a
sandbank, lay the body of her husband, wrapped in his plaid. He was buried
in the churchyard at Inverey, and the disconsolate widow with young
Donald, the only lasting proof of his love, retired to live in a tiny cottage
at Cnoc-Muircain.

Donald grew into a fine handsome lad and, like Kenneth M'Kenzie after him, entered the service of the laird of Invercauld as a shepherd. Now it so happened that this laird, Stewart, had no children save one daughter in her teens, as bonny a lass I believe as you would find in all Braemar. Soon it was a question of

> Come live with me and be my love,
> And we will all the pleasures prove
> That hills and valleys, dales and fields,
> Or woods or steepy mountain yields.

Invercauld was not best pleased with this turn of events, and the young couple set off up Glen Candlic, where Donald built a shieling for his young wife. Winter came, and she felt an interesting event approaching. It was a wild night, and Donald set off to find a skeelie woman to attend her. He was not long gone when three ugly old 'wivies' entered the hut and an heir was born to Donald, son of Fearchar Cam. The 'wivies' did all that was necessary and, on handing the child back to its mother,

'Let no mortal,' said the first,

'Touch the boy,' said the second,

'Till our return,' ended the third.

Morning came, and with it Donald and some of the good wives of Braemar. These were naturally disappointed that they had not been in time to assist at the birth, but were determined to bestow all sorts of attention on the child. The mother did all she could to keep her son from their touch, but in vain, and they had their way.

Some little time later, the mother and child were again left alone one evening in the shieling. In came the three witches, angrily demanding why their instructions had been disobeyed. She tried to explain, but they were not satisfied. Each one took the boy for a few moments in her arms and then, before parting, they held a long conversation to decide what 'weird' they should leave with him.

'The third part,' said one, 'of his fortune is taken away.'

'By the touch,' continued the second, 'of mortals.'

'But,' ended the third, significantly, 'he will prosper to the tenth generation.'

The boy was Fionnladh Mor. The old laird Stewart became reconciled to the family, and when he died his son-in-law became laird in his place; and from his father's name his descendants were known as M'Fearchar or Farquharson.

This is how the Farquharsons and Mackenzies came to Braemar and were united in marriage.

We do not hear of Mrs Beatrix M'Kenzie for another thirty years or more, but then her strong-minded, wilful character seems to have landed her in serious trouble. By now it was 1576 and the change of religion was taking place in Scotland. Strong beliefs were held by both sides and fierce disputes arose. The story is told in the words of the grandson of the famous Donald Farquharson of Castletown:

While Mary, our Queen, was in France, our nobles in Parliament, having promise of the church-lands and goods from the Reformers, passed an act to banish the parish priests (1560). Mr John Avignon (Owenson), priest in Braemar, would not obey, especially as this act was not subscribed by our Queen in Paris. He was a very pious, holy man, and was thought to have the spirit of prophecy. He threatened God's judgement on the first who laid hands upon him. Meanwhile, he preached with great zeal against the new religion. Beatrix Farquharson, daughter to Invercauld and sister to Donald Farquharson of Castletown – 'a bold woman', having cast out with the priest, arrived at kirk at the end of the first sermon. Some people, going out, told her the priest preached terribly against the new religion. 'Why,' says she, as she was coming in, 'don't you send him away with the rest, as the law orders?' 'We are afraid,' replied they, 'as he threatens God's judgement on him who lays hands upon him first.' 'I'll take my chance on that,' answered she, and went in and struck him on the shoulder. Then the hired people took hold of him, just as he was beginning Mass. After a little exhortation to stand firm to the doctrine he taught them, and teach it to their children, never to have any spiritual commerce with those new upstarts – self-commissioned heretics – he said that with time God would send them a priest commissioned by Jesus Christ and his Holy Church.

Those hired by the Government brought him down the way to Aberdeen. About forty of the oldest men followed him; among these was Donald of Castletown, above mentioned, my grandfather. At the march between the parish of Crathy and that of Braemar, Mr John told my grandfather to sit down, saying, 'I see by your tears you are sorry that I am banished, and I'll tell you something.'

The forty old men of the company sat close to hear what he would say. 'I am not content with your sister, Mrs M'Kenzie of Dalmore; and in token she has offended God, the hand that struck me today will rot and be cut from her shoulder before a year and a day pass.' This prophesy was spread far and near. The person concerned despised it. Some time thereafter, she felt an intolerable pain in her right arm; she sends to Aberdeen for a physician. The foreman and another were sent, and on their way they told their errand. They were told of the holy man's prophecy, and that what he

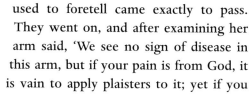

used to foretell came exactly to pass. They went on, and after examining her arm said, 'We see no sign of disease in this arm, but if your pain is from God, it is vain to apply plaisters to it; yet if you please, we will cut it off.' This she refused. Her arm turned blue and then black, and had such a stench that she got a room to herself. Before the year was ended, she was forced to cause it to be cut at her shoulder, and I heard my father, Lewis Farquharson, say he knew old men who saw her sleeve waving with the wind. I knew a

Curlews, by S. of G. Shee April 7. 1971

gentleman descended lineally of that woman, who told me and others he did not doubt the truth of that story. Very few in Braemar, come to any age since her time, have been ignorant or doubted of it, either Protestants or Catholics.

Although it is apparent from this dreadful story that Kenneth and Beatrix were still living at Dalmore in 1576, they must have prospered sufficiently to enable their son Robert to become a substantial landowner in Glenshee, for we know that by this time, or soon after, he was farming West Cuthill, the Town and Lands of Shanaval and the Burn of Elrick. He married, though we do not know the date, Janet 'Malcolmtosche' who must have been one of the M'Intoshes of Dalmunzie. This is born out by the fact that their son Patrick, who, like many of the family, took the alternative name of M'Comas (being descended from the original Thomas), was known as Patrick M'Kenzie of Stronalyne (of Dalmunzie). In 1605 Patrick married Isabel 'Malcolmtosche' who was almost certainly a relation, perhaps his cousin. It is when we come to his son Alexander M'Kenzie or M'Comas or M'Phatrick that details and concrete records begin to appear.

My grandmother, who in 1889, wrote a careful and detailed account of the

M'Kenzies, takes up the tale:

> In 1637 Alexander M'Kenzie, alias Wilsone, and his son John and Janet Robertstone his wife, received the charter of the lands etc. of Tomb in Glenshee from Alex Farquharson of Allanquhoich in Braemar. The charter enumerates that Duncan M'Kenzie, alias M'Comas, in Bray of Mar is attorney for the said John Wilsone and John M'Kenzie, alias M'Comas, in Dallmoir in Bray Mar is a witness.
>
> In 1665 sasine was granted to Duncan M'Kenzie, alias Wilsone, of the lands of Tomb then occupied by him, and there is still today a lintel over the back door of the house which bears the inscription 'DMK 1668 EM' and marks the date of his marriage and setting up house at Tomb.

But it is from Duncan's 'own brother' Robert that we are descended, and my grandmother wrote that in 1671 a contract of marriage was drawn up between this Robert and Jennet, eldest daughter of John Robertsone of Pettegowin. She had the original contract in front of her as she wrote, and states that 'all the parties to Robert's marriage contract signed their own names in good individual hands, and they are as follows:

> Robert M'Kenzie, John Robertson; Alex Robertsone (of Straloch), Robert M'Kenzie (of Runavey) and Kenneth his son and Duncan M'Kenzie of Tomb.

Robert M'Kenzie seems to have been a clever and capable man, one of those who are able to lend rather than compelled to borrow, and in 1684, while still living in Glenbeg, he had a mortgage on the lands of Crandart for 2500 merks from Thomas M'Intosh (or M'Combie), then of Fortar and Crandart. Ten years later, he granted the discharge of the mortgage, being then 'in Crandart', and there is still existing Lord Ogilvie's receipt for his rent in the following year, 'twa hundreth and fourscore punds Scots for the whole Mains of Crandart and Delanemer and Glenbrachie'. By 1699, however, he had become tacksman, not just yearly tenant, for in 1710 we have his renunciation of 'all and hail my possession of Crandart ... together with the glen called Glenbrachtye ... together with that glen or corrie called Glascorriebegg, likewise possessed by me ... conforme to the Tack. dated at Banff the sixteen day of March 1699 yeares ... I oblige me to flitt and remove myself, wyfe, bairns and servants, family, goods and gear ... against the said term of Whitsunday next to come ... dated at Kerrymure 19th Jan 1710'. Two years later we find him 'sometime in Crandart now in Finegand' and receiving for himself and Paul M'Kenzie his only son their charter of Finegand from the representatives of the late Robert Small (a brother of Small of Dirnanean), its previous owner.

But before passing on to Finegand, let me give you the text of a letter received by Paul M'Kenzie (or Wilsone) while still at Crandart. It throws a fascinating light on the customs of the time and Paul's personal relationship with his neighbours. It is addressed 'To Paull Wilsone. These with Caire', and was folded with unusual neatness and delicacy:

Ballochbuy, June the 23rd, 1710.

Sir, – Charles Farquharson, Tom, spoke to me the other day on your account, and assured me that ye would afford me some oxen to our saw milln for a whyll, upon condition that I were friendly in caise your cattell sometyme com in over to my Glens of Cariosowe, and he and I accorded and in your behalf he promised two plewmell one week and other two plewmell for a second week, and I assured him that I should give your cattell no trouble although they came in myn or my herd's ways, and that thos I gott for working should be taken good caire and well grassed. The designe of our having two plewmell att once is that on pleuch relieves the other, day or yokeing about, and those out of the yoke are grasing, so that att the week's end ye will never perceive them on whit the worse nor so much as know that they were ever wrought. My herd yesterday brought down some of your cattell by way of mistake, thinking that they belonged to Corribaiach, so that ye must cause your herds show myn all your cattell that haunts my bounds, and he will not trouble them when he drivs others. Deliver two plewmell to my herd on Monday com eight days, being the 3rd of July, and they shall be returned in the end of the week and the other two brought down when they go home. I would keep non of these heer at the tyme in caise you should not have thought it proper, therefor has returned them with the bearer. This being all (waiting your answer).

Sir, your Friend and Servant.

A. Farquharsone.

Robert M'Kenzie appears to have lived to a good old age, as in 1721 an agreement was made between him and his feudal superior the Duke of Athole, commutiug his personal service 'commonly known as Hosting, Hawking, Watching or Warding'.

However, we know from other correspondence that by 1729 Paul had entered into possession of Finegand. He was married to Marjorie Farquharson and had several sons of whom the eldest, Alexander, succeeded his father at Finegand in 1738. In 1725 he had married Grizell Robertson and by her had had several children, Colin, Alexander, John and Janet. Colin, the eldest, married, on January 3rd 1755 Jean, eldest daughter of Patrick Small of Leanoch and sister of Major-General John Small, and on his marriage his father retired from Finegand and he became the laird.

He had two sons, Alexander, born in 1755, and Patrick, born in 1758, but it seems that, after the birth of her second son, Mrs Mackenzie's health began to fail, and my grandmother in 1889 still had the prescription which Dr James Smyth of Perth recommended for her beneWt. Bleeding, emetics and blisters were among the list of remedies for her severe headaches, and to counteract the inevitable weakness which followed, a frequent spoonful of 'cordial' was required, while to heal the blisters kail blades rubbed with fresh butter were recommended.

I am sorry to have to tell you that these primitive measures proved less successful than the kindly Dr Smyth had hoped, and in 1763 the patient passed quietly away, leaving her two small sons motherless.

Not long afterwards, Colin married again, this time to Kitty, third daughter of Andrew Rattray of Dalrulzion. However, he does not seem to have had the careful disposition of his ancestor Robert, for in 1770 he sold the lands of Cronaherie and others in Glenbeg which had for so long formed part of the Finegand estate. Probably under the influence of his new wife, he purchased a house near Coupar Angus, but this move to a kinder climate was of no avail. His health was failing and in two years he was gone – leaving his affairs in some disarray.

On his move to Coupar Angus he had let Finegand to Alexander, son of John Robertson of Cray, and this had proved to be an unfortunate choice. On his death, litigation started between the young laird and his tenant, resulting in 'letters of horning' being issued against Robertson for three years' rent. Robertson, however, seemed as impervious to 'three several blasts of the Horn at the Market Cross of Edinburgh', denouncing him as His Majesty's Rebel as he was to 'Several knocks given on the most patent door of his principal dwelling-house'. By now he had left home but 'as he still dayley haunts and frequents Kirk, Market and other publick and private places within Scotland as if he were a free person and in high contempt of us, our Authority and Law and in evil example to others', Letters of Caption were issued and he was arrested, though at the insistence of Colin's widow he was released on a promise to pay the arrears of rent.

Meanwhile, as the two young brothers, Alexander and Patrick, struggled successfully with these problems (Alexander's hair was grey at the age of twenty), the Duke of Athole took a kindly interest in them and tried to persuade Alexander, who was six feet four inches in height and very good-looking, to take a commission in his Regiment of Athole Highlanders. Alexander's heart, however, was set on the Church, and he refused, but Patrick, as fine a looking man as his brother, gladly accepted, and the year 1779 saw one brother Chaplain and the other Ensign in the 77th Athole Highlanders.

The Rev. Alex. Mackenzie

For the next five years the Regiment served mainly in Ireland, but in 1783 it was disbanded and the men returned to their homes. Patrick enlisted in the 1st Royals and Alexander found his way to India, where he was for a time Chaplain to the Earl of Eglintoun. He returned in the ship of Admiral Gell who recommended him to Mr Wilkinson, the Vicar of Sheffield. The two clerics seem to have got on well, for in 1789 Mr M'Kenzie was appointed Incumbent of St Paul's Church in Sheffield, where he remained, loved and respected by all, until his death in 1816.

He was an imposing figure in rustling gown and black knee-breeches as he strode down 'M'Kenzie's Walk' to his church on a Sunday morning, and a fine preacher as reported by a local historian: 'Hear him but reason in divinity and you would vow he was born a Prelate'.

Yet, at the same time he was a genial and friendly man who enjoyed life to the full. Regular supplies of whisky from the old country had to be arranged and delivered, and its condition and safe carriage were from time to time the subject of correspondence with his tenant. Like all Highlanders, he loved to dance, and this little story told to my grandmother may help us to understand the affection that the people of Sheffield had for him:

October 1889.

Mr M'Kenzie of St Paul's was before my time; but I have often heard my late father speak of him as a tall, dignified but genial man. My father used to tell the following story: Mr Sutton, the Vicar of Sheffield, after he became 'converted', took upon himself to remonstrate with Mr M'Kenzie for attending such worldly places of amusement as Assembly Rooms, and sometimes joining in a dance. 'It is all very well for you, Sutton,' said Mr M'Kenzie, 'but then you are lame and cannot dance. But I can, and what is more, if I think proper, I shall!'

On 31st January 1788, he married Miss Margaret Smith, a rich and charming young lady. They had three children, but then in the family bible come two thick black lines and the sad entry, 'On Thursday 11th July at 4 o'clock in ye morning I became a most wretched widower and my infant children motherless. AM'. Years later, in 1801, he married Miss Sarah Wilson and on 15th December 1806 their only child, Mary-Anne, was born. There were no grand-children of the first marriage and she was the last of the Finegand Mackenzies, but in 1828 she married William Smith of Barnes Hall and became the mother of a fine family of ten sons and three daughters. Her eldest son, Alexander Mackenzie Smith, was laird from the date of her death in 1874 until 1907, and her grandson, William Mackenzie Smith, from 1907 to 1957, when the present family company was formed.

From 1772 until 1957, a period of 185 years, there were only four lairds of Finegand:

Alexander M'Kenzie	1772–1816
Mary-Anne Mackenzie	1816–1874
Alexander Mackenzie Smith	1874–1907
William Mackenzie Smith	1907–1957

While Alexander lived and tended his flock in Sheffield, his brother Patrick was rising steadily in his chosen profession. In 1793, he was present at the defence of Toulon, where he received three severe wounds in a sortie made by the garrison. In 1794, he served in the force which took part in the descent on Corsica.

He was present at the storming of the Convention Redoubt and also at the siege of Calvi where he was again wounded. In 1798, he was on the Staff in the West Indies and present at the taking of Surinam. On 23rd January 1800, he was promoted Major in the famous 43rd Light Infantry with which he served until 1804, when he was made Lietenant-Colonel in the 81st Regiment; Colonel 4th June 1813. He served for some years in the Peninsula, and after forty-two years' service was promoted to the rank of Major-General. He died unmarried on 7th March 1820, aged sixty-two years.

Sub-Lieutenant Patrick Mackenzie Smith, Bombay 1945

The last laird, Billy, was a distinguished soldier and even more disinguished lawyer. He commanded his Regiment, the Queen's Own Yorkshire Dragoons, in the 1914-18 war and was awarded the DSO and Mentioned in Despatches by Earl Haig. He had no children, but five of his brothers also served in France, and ten of his nephews fought in the Second World War. Some were decorated, some were wounded, but in the end we all came home except John. In 1947 Billy crowned a successful legal career by becoming President of the Law Society.

From the foregoing, perhaps you are beginning to think that the Mackenzies and Mackenzie Smiths were all paragons of virtue and honest, useful citizens. It was not always so, and to set the record straight and end this chapter on a lighter note, here are one or two stories of an earlier and more disreputable cousin from Braemar, as told by John Grant:

Gilleasbuig MacCoinnich, alias Gilleasbuig Urrasach, that is Archibald M'Kenzie, alias Archibald the Proud or the Bold, was a small person, well shaped and with a ruddy face and light brown hair. For his size he was wonderfully strong, and all life, activity and vigour. No-one in Braemar knew better how to manage the claymore, targe and dirk, as no-one with pistol or gun could so surely hit a given mark. In character he was remarkable for cunning, contempt of hardship and fatigue, inflexibility of purpose, great presence of mind in extreme dangers, unbending fidelity to his chief, and the most implacable enmity to his foes. His daring surpassed belief and his pride seemed ridiculous. He could never bear to be employed in agricultural labour, or to be treated like any ordinary countryman. He had ever a craving to act the gentleman and appear more than what he was. When

Maj. Gen. Patrick Mckenzie, by Henry Edridge (*Sheffield Galleries & Museums Trust*)

he drank his *brochan* or *sowens*, when he supped his porridge and milk, when he dined on kail or brose, in fine, whatever he had to eat, he must needs be served on table-cloth, with cover, knife and fork, whether he had any use for them or not, or whether he was in company or alone. He would not stir beyond the threshold without being armed to the teeth, and beside the ordinary complement of gun, broadsword, dirk, targe, a pair of pistols, and a skian dubh stuck in the garter of each hose, he carried one in the sleeve of each arm. This was to prevent a surprise in whatever position or state the enemy might find him, and to assure an arm offensive, even when fallen or taken at close quarters by an enemy of greater personal strength. He would, at times, when sharpening his sword, dirk or skians, deign to survey the labours on his croft, and when he thought the blades sufficiently whetted, he would unceremoniously go and drive them into his mother's legs as she stooped to her toil. If she complained of the excessive pain caused by this operation, her dutiful son would continue his sharpening, concluding that the edge was not sufficiently restored. But if the maternal complaint was not great, he would cease, persuaded the edge was so fine that it cut cleanly and without causing pain.

In his early years, Gillespie happened to be employed, with a number of his countrymen and some of the Gairnside folks, in driving wood south through Glenshee. As chance would have it, just as they were descending into the Glen where the peat road strikes off scrambling up the hillside, a great band of the Glenshee men with their horses and currachs were trudging up the brae on the way for a load of peats. Now, a kind of petty wordy war has existed between the inhabitants of both glens from time immemorial, and the Glenshee men, seeing they were numerically superior to the wood-drivers, began to pour out abuse on the heads of the unfortunate company passing below. None of the offended party dared budge or give a return in kind, but Gillespie, stung to the quick, could not endure their insults. With a dirk in one hand and a skian in the other, he sprang up the brae and, without a word, beginning at the last horse and ending with the first, he cut the girths and tumbled the currachs onto the ground. After completing this exploit to his satisfaction, he leaped onto a little hillock and cried out, 'Now men, after this say nothing of the Gairnside and Braemar men, even though you see they are fewer in number than you are, for if ever I hear again what I have heard today, I'll cut up every one of you as I have today cut your horses' girths.'

Not long after this, Gillespie, in exactly the same employment, happened alone to pass through Glenshee. As he was crossing the Blackwater by the ford, a party of countrymen, coming from the opposite direction, met him midways in the stream. One of them, as he went by, gave a sounding thwack with his bludgeon to Gillespie's horse. The horse leaped to the farther side. Flame sparkled in Gillespie's eyes and his dirk flashed over his head. All the ocean of water, thrown by his horse's feet like a shroud of mercy in his face and over his head, did but enkindle his ire. He turned smartly round and, with a dig of his dirk, opened the calf of one of his malefactor's legs. This was not enough and both went floundering through the water to the bank. The wounded man called his companions to the rescue. A desperate struggle ensued, Gillespie struck right and left, inflicting wounds on several of the party, and stretching him who had dared to violate his horse on the ground. But the dirk, in the long run, is no match for seven or eight bludgeons; and so it appeared on this occasion, for Gillespie in his turn rolled senseless beside his fallen enemy. The victors, believing both to be dead, took flight, pursued by Old Nick and a guilty conscience.

But a Samaritan, whose forefathers, by progress of events and changes of time, had come to dwell in Glenshee, happening to come that way, perceived that there yet remained a small spark of life in the deserted fallen. He had them both conveyed to his house, one installed in a bed in the *but* end, the other in the *ben*, and their wounds and bruises attended to. Time breathed favourably on the two worthies, and in the lapse of four days, retored part of their former strength.. The good man with his family went out one day to his field labours, leaving the doors unbarred and his house tenanted by Gillespie and his foe. The good wife about mid-day came home to prepare the dinner. She pushed the outer door open, but the sight that met her eyes made her start with a cry of horror. Gillespie, bare naked, crawling on all fours, seamed with scars, black and blue with bruises, his body and limbs swollen all over, groaning with pain, and his dirk between his teeth, had got midway down the passage on his way to settle the account between himself and the wounded Glenshee man. He was forced to bed, and watched afterwards, and as soon as he could be removed his host took care to have him conveyed to Braemar.

Black Grouse
at 'lek'

4 *The Royal Route to Deeside*

new Larch.

Ever since Malcolm Canmore built himself a hunting lodge at Braemar in 1059 and took his fair wife Margaret there to share his sport, the valley of the Shee has been frequented by travellers of all degrees, from the occupant of the throne to the humblest of drovers and cairds.

For centuries, the road was no more than a grassy track, but then, in 1748, work started on the military road from Blairgowrie to Braemar.

General Wade had retired eight years before, but such had been his fame and success as a road-builder that for many years to come all the military roads and bridges in Scotland were built to his design, and the beautiful old stone bridge at the Spital is one of many in Scotland which are a tribute to the artistic skill of this great engineer.

His roads were 16 feet wide and were built as close to the Roman pattern as the nature of the country would allow. They were laid out to avoid any place where there might be an ambush though, as you will read in another chapter, this was not always successful. Every season there were anything from 200 to 500 soldiers employed on the work. Privates received 6*d*. (2p) per day and sub-alterns in charge of parties 2*s*. 6*d*. (12p).

Although undoubtedly a technical success, the new road caused a storm of local opposition, for it was declared that the metalled surface would be cruelly hard on the unshod feet of men and horses.

The part that I know best lies between Blairgowrie and the Cairnwell, and every hill and corner (and there are plenty of both) has a tale to tell.

A mile north of Blairgowrie is the village of Rattray, and just above this is Craighall, the seat of the Clerk-Rattrays. This fine old house was visited by Sir Walter Scott who acknowledged to the laird that it was the origin of his

General George Wade.

Tullyveolan. Rose Bradwardine's room is thought to be in the little turret with pinnacles.

Tradition says that, in the reign of King James V, John Stewart, third Earl of Athole, married Grizel Rattray, only daughter of Sir John Rattray, and expected to acquire the property. Sir John, however, married again and by his second wife had two sons and a daughter. As the years passed, the earl's feelings of disappointment deepened, and at length he sent an armed band of his retainers who attacked the castle and slew all the inhabitants, including Sir John and one of his sons. A devoted nurse, however, managed to escape with the other son and made her way to Dundee. The earl took possession of the property, but some years later the rightful heir appeared and claimed the barony. The influence of the earl was so great in Perth, where he had a town house, that the authorities refused to carry out the proper legal processes, but King James arranged for this to be done in Dundee, and young Rattray was restored to his estate.

The family supported Montrose in his war with the Covenanting army, and it is said that on one occasion General Bailey attacked the house with cannon in order to persuade the laird to disclose Montrose's whereabouts. The laird, however, had wisely absented himself from the house and only an old man-servant named Andrew could be found. This brave old man refused to give any information as to where his master had gone, and as a reward for his loyalty he was thrown over the cliff into the river.

The events of the next war a hundred years later proved happier for the Rattrays. After the battle of Culloden, the house was searched for fugitive Jacobites, but this time all escaped by hiding down the cliff below the house. The laird's younger brother also escaped death by a lucky chance and the quick wits of his lawyer. He had survived the battle but, like my ancestor John Scott,* had been captured afterwards. Scott was hanged, but young Rattray was sent for trial in Edinburgh. He was convicted and sentenced to death, but he happened to be an outstanding young golfer and his counsel, knowing that the judge also was a keen golfer, pleaded persuasively that it would be a real tragedy and an irreparable loss to the game if his young client were to be hanged. The judge readily agreed that this would indeed be the case and Rattray was immediately released.

A little further on, between Craighall and Bridge of Cally, is a property known as Mause which has a well-known ghost story attached to it – the ghost in this case being a four-footed one, a collie (though some say a fox to which no dog would give chase). This collie (or fox) appeared at night to the farmer at Mause and, being miraculously able to speak, urged him to remove the body of a cattle drover who had been murdered on his way home from market with the proceeds of the sale in his pocket. The ghost's repeated request was 'bury the baines', and it described where these were to be found. The resulting search uncovered the bones in a shallow grave beside the river and they were removed and re-buried in Blairgowrie churchyard. With its mission accomplished, the dog (or fox) must

---

* *John Scott was the grandson of James Scott, Duke of Monmouth, beheaded by his uncle James II after the Battle of Sedgemoor. He was the great-grandfather of Dr Alexander Scott, Nelson's chaplain at Trafalgar.*

have been completely satisfied, for my niece, who lives at Mause, assures me that it has never been seen since.

Bridge of Cally means 'Bridge of the Skirts', so called because it was for many generations the home of an order of monks. Here the road divides, left for Strathardle and Pitlochry and right for Glenshee and Braemar.

It is the right-hand road that we must take, and soon we come to Persie. Here there was, in the late seventeen hundreds, a Chapel of Ease where my great-great-grandfather, Alexander Mackenzie, preached many a sermon before he went out to India. But the best remembered minister of Persie is the Reverend John Duncan, known in 1830 as 'Rabbi Duncan' because of his skill in languages, particularly Hebrew. He was undoubtedly a brilliant scholar, so it is perhaps a little sad that he is remembered more for his eccentricity and absent-minded ways than for his learning.

Red Grouse ♂

He was, like many of his brethren, fond of snuff, and it is said that one day, on his way to a wedding, he decided that he would take a pinch. He took out his mull but, as there was a stiff breeze blowing in his face, he turned his pony round to protect the contents. He took his snuff and set off again, but as he had forgotten to turn his pony a second time, he soon arrived back at his lodgings, quite unconscious of the fact that he had not conducted the wedding ceremony.

On another occasion, he went to preach in a neighbouring parish and, on his arrival at the manse on a winter's afternoon, was shown to his bedroom to remove his muddy boots. When supper was announced and he had not re-appeared it was discovered that, absorbed in thought and unconscious of time, he had got undressed, gone to bed and fallen fast asleep.

In spite of these little lapses of memory, his Highland flock were very fond of him and showed him much kindness. He lodged a mile or two from the church and used to ride over on Sunday mornings, but as he always forgot his gloves, even in winter, his hands were numb with cold when he arrived at church. Noticing this, kindly members of the congregation would press their own upon him. When he left Persie, fifteen pairs were found in the pulpit.

One of the pupils who studied under him at the Free Church College recalled that one day Duncan had written some Hebrew sentences on the blackboard but had forgotten his pointer. He asked for the loan of a stick and was given a smart cane. After the lesson was over, he left the college carrying it in his hand. When this was pointed out to the student who had lent the cane, he replied cheerfully, 'Oh, that's all right! I knew what he would do and I lent him yours!'

The Reverend John Duncan left Persie for Milton Church in Glasgow in 1836 and in 1840 Aberdeen University, his alma mater, conferred on him the degree of LL.D.

Across the valley from Persie is the hill known as Kingseat, from which tradition says the ancient Scottish kings used to watch the boar hunts which were for so long a favourite sport in the Highlands.

And so, on up the Glen to Dalrulzion where, for many years, there was a petrol station. When I returned to the Glen in 1953, the proprietor was named McDowel. He was an elderly man who sat all day hunched over the financial papers, staring through a pair of spectacles crookedly and precariously balanced

Finegand, 1965

on the end of his nose. There were few cars on the road then and this absorbing study was seldom interrupted by requests for petrol, with the result that the old man was the undisputed stockmarket expert for miles around. I knew landowners with many thousands of acres who travelled to Dalrulzion, whether they needed petrol or not, just to listen to his wisdom, and they were never disappointed. McDowel died at the age of ninety and left a considerable fortune to his heirs.

Glenshee itself, wild, beautiful Glen of the Fairies, starts at the head of the Lair Brae. There, down to your right, opposite Dalnaglar Castle, is an area of low-lying ground known as Tynellan, in the middle of which is the roofless ruin of a cottage said to have been for many years the home of John Farquharson, the finest rifle shot in the world – yes, I mean *the world*, and the most famous poacher in Perthshire. So varied and colourful were his adventures that I have devoted a whole chapter to them.

Opposite Tynellan, and a few yards from the road, is the famous Clach-na-Coileach, and then a mile further on is Finegand, bought by Robert Mackenzie in 1712 and owned by my family ever since. The name is derived from the Gaelic *Feigh-nan-Ceann*, the Hollow of the Heads, and there is a well-known story of how this name came about. We are told that:

No clan was so noted for lording it over their weak neighbours as the Campbells. Formerly they were wont to come the rounds of Glenshee to extract tribute, 'in goodlie array', riding on ponies, to the heads of which bells were fixed, that the people, thus warned, might, without more trouble to my gents, bring forth their contributions. Andrew Stewart, farmer at Drumforkat, by no means admired this sort of proceeding – more to the liking of the Campbells than to the profit of his country, and gathering a few gallant fellows, he fell on a party of the insolent oppressors, cut off their heads and rolled them into a burn, still called *Feigh-nan-Ceann* (the Hollow of the Heads). For this brave deed Stewart had to fly. Closely pursued, he entered a mill, exchanged his clothes for a dusty suit of the miller's, and was calmly picking away at the millstone when those in search of him arrived.

'Did anyone enter here a little while ago?' was demanded.

'There is no-one here,' Stewart made ready reply, 'but the miller.'

And they passed on. He and his descendants have therefore ever since been called Miller. After this narrow escape, he took a fancy to the scenery of Braemar, as much more the thing than that of Glenshee, and bethought himself he would honour it by removing his household gods thither.

At Corrydon, on the site of the present house, there was formerly a very humble cottage inhabited by an old widow. She was poor and wretched and bent and ugly, and every day as the coach travelled up to Braemar she would come to the door of her cottage to see it pass by. One day, among the travellers, there was a rich and extremely smart middle-aged man. The others on the coach were somewhat in awe of such a grand personage, but when the coach reached Corrydon their awe turned to amazement. The grand gentleman called in an imperious voice for the driver to stop. Jumping down from his seat, he ran to the old woman and embraced her tenderly. He then returned to the coach, and in reply to the enquiring glances of his fellow passengers he exclaimed in a voice in which happiness was mixed with pride, 'That's my mother!'

Beauty, we all know, is in the eye of the beholder, and whatever the old widow appeared to the world, she was surely to her son the lovely young woman he remembered as a child.

At the head of the Glen is the Spital of Glenshee which is so called from the hospice, or hospital, which stood there very many years ago. The word has a Latin origin and means literally 'apartments for strangers', so it was evidently more of an inn, as it is now, than a hospital. The site was well chosen on the busy route from Perth to Braemar just where the road begins to climb steeply up Glenbeg to the Cairnwell. To travel over this road in winter must have been hazardous and exhausting, and from the name Shanspital on the Clunie we know that there was a hospice on the other side of the pass as well. It has been suggested, and seems likely, that these two inns were built and maintained by a religious order of monks similar to that of St Bernard. Whether this is so or not, the Spital of Glenshee must have been a place of some importance, for there is at least one Charter in existence signed there by King Robert II.

Above the Spital the Glen divides, with Glenlochsie and Glentaitneach running due north and Glenbeg north-east to the Cairnwell and Braemar. Where the road crosses the Cairnwell there was for a hundred and fifty years the famous landmark known as The Devil's Elbow. It was not part of the original military road which ran much further up the hillside, but owed its existence to an enterprising brother and sister partnership. When Charles Watson, proprietor of the Invercauld Arms in Braemar, died, his sister, Mrs Clarke of Invergelder, took over the hotel in May 1829. At the same time her brother, Thomas Watson, was hotel-keeper at the Spital of Glenshee. Brother and sister hit on the idea of starting a coach service from Perth to Braemar but, as parts of the old military road over the Cairnwell were not suitable for a coach, they set about improving it at their own expense, and so The Devil's Elbow was created. The coach service must have been a great success for it continued from 1829 to 1922, when it was the last coach running anywhere in Britain.

My father told me that so steep was the famous double hairpin bend that the only way the early cars could negotiate it was in reverse, for this was, of course, the lowest gear. There was also a well just below the bend so that boiling radiators could be filled after the long journey up Glenbeg, and in preparation for the daunting task ahead.

5 The Upper Glens

Glenshee extends for about two miles north of the Spital to a point called Sheneval, near the junction of the two valleys, Glenlochsie and Glentaitneach, or the Pleasant Vale. This district was well populated two hundred years ago by families of MacIntoshes, Mackenzies, Lamonts, Lyons and Grants, but now there are only heaps of stones and clumps of birch where once there were homesteads for over a score of tenants.

One of these birches is known as 'M'Kenzie's Tree'. It marks the site of a little incident which demonstrates the independence and strength of character of the Highlander and justifies the ancient motto 'What I have I hold'. M'Kenzie of Cuthill had in some way offended one of the lairds of Strathardle and my grandmother, writing in 1889, quotes the old legend.

Once on a time Baron Roy of Balvarron in Strathardle sent an officer and twelve armed retainers to Cuthill for the purpose of taking M'Kenzie of Cuthill down to Balvarron. M'Kenzie was engaged in making his haystack when he saw Baron Roy's men come down the opposite hill. Having asked his servant to bring his bow and arrows, he proceeded with his work. Roy's men approached to within speaking distance, when the officer, standing against a tree, shouted that if M'Kenzie was at home Baron Roy wished to see him. M'Kenzie in reply shot an arrow which entered the tree against which the officer stood close to the officer's head, and at the same time M'Kenzie cried out that if one of them moved a step nearer the next arrow should enter his heart, that he was M'Kenzie, but he was busy with his own affairs, and that Baron Roy must come to Cuthill if he wished to see him. The officer and his men ventured no further, but returned to Balvarron as they had come.

On the south side of the Lochsie one can still see the foundation lines of the old castle of Dalmunzie, for so long the home of the MacIntoshes, but of the castle itself nothing remains.

In Glenbeg too, there are still traces of past cultivation and occupancy by many families, which we know included Ramsays and M'Kenzies. At first glance one might say what a bleak and uninteresting glen this is – just a little stream bordered by a few hundred yards of rough pasture, and on either side the steep hills covered with rocks and heather. With the exception of a few birches at the lower end, and here and there a rowan planted to ward off the evil spirits, there is not a tree to be seen. Yet, bare and empty as it now seems, it was once, long ago, a scene of busy Highland life, studded with heather-thatched dwellings round which the children played and where the scent of peat smoke filled the air. On both sides of the valley, half a mile or so from the Rhidorrach, now the only inhabited house in Glenbeg, there can still be seen green mounds of what were once houses and steadings, occupied for hundreds of years by the hardiest race of men and women in Europe. On the eastern slope, by the side of the Allanduie Burn, the outline of the house and offices of a large grazing called Cronaherie is still visible, along with the track of a water-course leading from a pool in the burn to the steading. A mountain spring of ice-cold water, called 'the spring on which the sun never shone', flows from the southern bank and shows why the site of the farm was chosen. The stack-yard terraces can also be distinguished, and the remains of this holding are of special interest to me because it was for so many years owned and farmed by generations of M'Kenzies.

Some three hundred yards to the south of Cronaherie, and by the side of another burn, the remains of another dwelling can be seen. This was called Laganagriene (the hollow of the bones) and a mile and a half north of Cronaherie there was another shieling called Gormel (the green hill); but about two hundred

Black houses

and fifty years ago this was overwhelmed by an avalanche, and the Ramsays who lived there had to make a wonderful escape in the middle of the night. On the opposite side of the valley from Cronaherie and not far above the road were one or two other houses, Laganamer (the trough-shaped hollow), Craigdearg (the red crag) and, on top of a steep bank, Clachnaherna or Clacherna (the burial place of the lairds).

Simple, even primitive, as these dwellings were, they were home to men and women whose daily toil still left time for a remarkably high level of education, evident from the marriage contract of Robert M'Kenzie, which I have already described.

Robert was succeeded in Cronaherie by his son-in-law, Alexander Ramsay, whose family remained tenants there for nearly two hundred years.

Alexander was the son of Ramsay of Tullimurdoch who had joined the Earl of Argyle and his Campbell followers in the treacherous burning of the 'Bonnie House of Airlie' in 1640. Soon after, however, the Ogilvies found their revenge. Ramsay was killed in a fight and his son Alexander was sought out at Tullimurdoch where he lived with his now widowed mother. When the Ogilvies arrived with the intention of carrying him off, he proposed to give himself up, but his high-spirited mother refused to allow this, saying she would rather see him dead than a prisoner in the hands of his enemies. With her encouragement, he decided to make his escape by night and, having killed one of the Ogilvies, he disappeared in the direction of the Blackwater. Knowing that he would be pursued with hounds, when he reached the river near Dalrulzion he made a gash in one of his hands and, with the blood, made a wide circle in the heather. He then leapt into the river and after wading upstream for some distance, emerged on the opposite bank. He continued his flight towards Strathardle where he found refuge in the hut of a friendly shepherd at a spot still known as 'Leabaidh Ramsay' or 'Ramsay's Bed'. Here he stayed for two days, but then learned that the pursuers were still on his track.

Again he took to the hills, and in time arrived at the Spital of Glenshee. Here he was again befriended, this time by a cobbler who tied an apron round him, put a black patch over one eye and a hammer and an old shoe into his hand, transforming him instantly into an apprentice. When the Ogilvies arrived, they failed to recognise him seated on a stool and busily mending the old shoe. Eventually, they gave up the search and Ramsay, feeling himself safe in Glenbeg, entered the service of Robert M'Kenzie of Cronaherie. It was a wise choice and must also have been a happy time, for he married M'Kenzie's daughter and eventually became tenant in his father-in-law's farm. He was always known as Alexander Greusaich, the shoemaker's Alexander. He died in 1702 and his tombstone can still be seen in the churchyard at the Spital.

One of the strangest and most romantic stories of the Glen concerns his daughter, who was considered to be a particularly attractive young woman. The son of a landowner in Strathardle had fallen in love with her, but the young man's father had other and probably more ambitious ideas, and did all he could to prevent the match. Persuasion seemed to be useless and eventually he resorted to a treacherous scheme. Pretending to consent to the marriage, he invited the young lady to accompany him to Dundee on the pretext of buying her wedding clothes and furnishings for her new home. Once there, he showed her the sights of the town and then suggested that they should visit one of the ships in the harbour. He had already made arrangements with the captain of the ship which was due to sail for the Mediterranean in the afternoon. Once aboard, Miss Ramsay was invited to the captain's cabin. Here the laird left her, saying he would return in a short time. An hour passed and he did not return. Feeling uneasy, she returned to the deck and there her anxiety turned to despair, for the ship was underway and sailing down the estuary of the Tay. She knew she had been betrayed and, separated from home, family and friends, was being carried she knew not where; but in her wildest dreams she could not have guessed what her future held in store for her.

When, eventually, the ship reached the Mediterranean she was taken ashore in Morocco and sold in the notorious slave market of the great capital city.

However, she was, as I have said, a beautiful girl and her appearance and her gentle manner gained her an entrance to the Palace. She was admitted to the Royal Harem and soon became the favourite wife of the Emperor, eventually being elevated to high rank and acquiring great influence at Court.

Some years later, the wicked laird who had betrayed her decided to pay a visit to the south of France, but his ship was driven off its course by a gale and was seized by Moorish pirates. The wheel of fortune was turning relentlessly, and the laird and his companions were, in their turn, taken ashore and sold in the same slave market.

As she passed through the streets, the Empress, for such the daughter of Ramsay of Cronaherie had now become, saw this group of Scotsmen and ordered that they should be brought to the Palace. To her intense amazement she recognised her cruel betrayer, but instead of seeking revenge, such was her gentle nature that she ordered their release and sent them home laden with gifts. Before leaving, the laird, as spokesman for the party, asked what they could do to show their gratitude, when she revealed her identity and said that many times she had sat at his table, that he had treated her with the utmost cruelty, but she bore him no ill-will.

Some years later, two of her sons, described as Princes of Morocco, arrived in Dundee intending to seek out their mother's family in Glenbeg and bearing gifts for them, but unfortunately it was the time of the great Rebellion and it was considered too dangerous for foreigners to venture into the Highlands and they had to return with their mission unfulfilled.

But let us return from the splendour of Morocco to the simplicity of Glenshee, where it has been remarked that the real wealth of these hardy and independent men lay in the fewness of their wants, and where it is certain that in their pastoral lives they were almost entirely self-sufficient. Clothes were made from the wool of their own sheep, and in the long winter evenings round the fireside the singing and stories were accompanied by the soft whirr of the spinning wheel. The main garment of the ordinary folk was the belted plaid and later the short kilt or philabeg, but coats and waistcoats were also worn and tailors went their rounds among the farms and shielings, and where they worked were included as members of the household.

Corn was grown, even in the upper glens, but harvesting was late and difficult and the grain had to be kiln dried before it could be eaten. Dr Johnson, who hated 'Scotchmen', once remarked that in England oats was the principal food of horses, but in Scotland it was the principal food of the men. This crude observation showed little understanding of the facts, for oatmeal and the milk of sheep or cows is a healthy and balanced diet, and on it the Highland drovers produced feats of endurance which would astonish even the trained athletes of today.

For centuries, Lanark Moor was the principal market-place for Blackface lambs which the northern farmers bought from the south-country breeders. The flockmasters did their own bargaining and, with their shepherds, walked from Glenshee to Edinburgh, a distance of 80 miles, in two stages. There they spent the night and the next day covered the remaining 50 miles. After completing their purchases, they returned home with the lambs by easy stages. By the end of the week they had walked some 260 miles, and this on a diet of oatmeal and milk.

brooding Oyster Catcher.

My great-grandfather for many years used to bring store cattle from Glenshee and other Perthshire glens to fatten on his rich Yorkshire pastures. These cattle were brought down by Highland drovers and the whole journey was made on foot. The round trip was 600 miles and the drovers carried nothing with them but a bag of oatmeal which they mixed with water and made into oatcakes which were cooked on stones heated by a stick fire. They never put up at a farmhouse but, wrapped in their plaids, slept every night in the open. On special occasions, or when conditions were more than usually harsh, the oatmeal was mixed with whisky instead of water, and this is an oatcake I strongly recommend.

Donald Ramsay of Cronaherie was living proof of the benefits of a frugal life. He was said to be a man of vigorous constitution and temperate habits whose motto was 'Drink little that you may drink long'. If ever he arrived home late from the hill or from a long journey he never allowed anyone to wait up for him, but just took a few mouthfuls of cold porridge and went to bed, and was astir before any of his family. It was his normal habit to retire at nine and rise at five. He died in 1842 at the age of ninety two. His father, John Ramsay, *The Duine*, a strong old man of ninety four, was killed by a falling stone while mending the roof of his lime kiln.

Yet, hardy and long-lived though the inhabitants of Glenshee undoubtedly were, they seem as children to those of the island of Jura where my father told me he had seen, in the burial ground at Ardlussa, the following remarkable inscription:

MARY M'CRAIN
Died in 1856, aged 128
Descendant of Gillour M'Crain, who kept one hundred and eighty
Christmases in his own house, and who died in the reign of Charles I

Unfortunately, we do not know how many Christmases Gillour M'Crain kept in other people's houses, so his exact age remains a mystery.

One of the Earls of Airlie was in the habit of staying a night or two when shooting in Glenisla at the farmhouse of one of his tenants. He arrived unexpectedly on one occasion at about mid-day and Mrs Stewart had no dinner prepared. In this emergency she quickly prepared a bowl of good stiff porridge and, with a jug of cream, set it before him. After his meal, the earl declared he had never had a better dinner. The person who told me this story suggested that he had had a long walk that morning and that 'hunger is the best sauce', but I think that would be unfair to the good Mrs Stewart and her excellent porridge.

Winter in the upper glens was a time of hardship for both man and beast. Many a little dwelling became drifted over in the night, and when the gudeman opened his door in the morning it was to find himself confronted by a white wall of snow. To cut a way out would mean filling the house with melting snow, and the usual method adopted was to push a child armed with a shovel up the chimney, always built conveniently wide, who proceeded to dig a track, or even sometimes a tunnel, to the door.

For six months each year the sheep were sent down to the lower districts of Perthshire and Forfarshire. This was an expensive exercise, but if it had not been done serious losses would certainly have resulted, and here I must tell you of the different behaviour of sheep and deer in a snowstorm and why, in most cases, the deer will survive and the sheep will perish. In these conditions the deer will face the storm and find their way to some ridge or exposed part of the hill which has been swept clear of snow by the wind. Here, no matter how fierce the storm or intense the cold, they will stay, for some strong instinct tells them that, however they suffer, they are safer here than in some sheltered hollow where surely they would be covered by the snow and smothered. Sheep on the other hand, simple stupid creatures quite unlike the deer, will turn their backs on the storm and walk slowly before it until they come to some obstacle – a stone, a wall or a cliff face – and here they will stop. As the drift builds up against the obstacle they inevitably become covered. Then, after the storm, it is the shepherd's job to search the hill with his dogs and a long pole which he thrusts into every drift in the hope of feeling some small movement. If he is lucky he must then dig, and dig, and dig.

I have told you that I lost fifty seven ewes in one night in such a storm, and I have heard that a farmer in Glenbeg lost, again in one night, no less than five hundred sheep and five horses.

Before the introduction of turnips to the glens in about 1780, the only winter feed was a meagre crop of hay and most of the cattle were sent away to the Carse of Gowrie where they were fed on straw. This was a poor diet, but it kept them alive and no charge was made for it as the straw was converted to valuable manure for the arable ground. In the spring the cattle, often pitifully thin, returned to the mountain pastures to be fattened for market. I have heard it said that some of the cattle wintered in the glens were so weak in the spring that they were unable to make the journey to the summer shielings and had to be taken out on sledges.

But if the winter was harsh and cruel, the beauty and the joy of spring and summer made up for it a thousand times. As in all mountain districts, spring comes late to the glens, but when it comes it seems to arrive overnight. One morning you will wake up and find that the cold north wind has given way to a gentle breeze from the south. High up in the sky you may see wedges of geese flying north to their nesting grounds and hear their faint incessant clamour. Peewits, curlews and oyster-catchers will arrive and the melting snow fills the river with water of the palest, purest green you have ever seen. This was indeed the happiest and the busiest time of the year. The shepherds made their way down to the lower ground and returned slowly with their flocks. Lambing started and with it the constant war against the mountain foxes, so numerous in some parts that the sheep were enclosed at night in folds with high stone walls.

Greylag Geese

Later in the summer, whole families moved up to the summer shielings where the sheep and cattle grazed. They lived in simple shelters to which all the necessities of life were brought on the backs of ponies – cooking pots, dishes, fuel, food supplies and even spinning wheels. The bed boxes, which were left in the shiels throughout the winter, were annually filled with fresh heather for a mattress. The method was to cut a supply of heather and allow it to dry, then cut it into lengths of about nine inches and pack it tightly into the boxes with the flowers uppermost, so making a soft and comfortable bed.

This again was a happy, carefree time; a time of laughter and song and love-making, and the most poignant description we have of it is from Jane Elliot in her lament 'The Flowers of the Forest'. I know that in every war men must die and women must weep, but I know of no other ballad which tells so vividly of the emptiness left behind by death.

Another job which the men had to do while the women and girls were tending the sheep was cutting the peats. This was the only fuel in the glens and it had to be cut and dried in the summer for burning in the winter. When properly dried it makes a beautiful hot fire and the smell of the peat reek is something which one can never forget, and the memory of which the Scots and Irish have carried with them to the ends of the earth. It reminds me of something I was once told by a Canadian Indian in Quebec. I believe there is no race on earth so wonderfully in tune with their natural surroundings as the North American Indian. Sitting Bull, Running Deer, Laughing Water, even their names echo their love of the world around them, and they have an understanding of the simple things of life which we cannot match. When an Indian goes on a long journey or on the warpath he knows he will be separated from all the things he loves, his squaw, his home and his children, and to remind himself of them he takes a small medicine bag and in it four or five objects, each with a different smell. He does not take things to look at or to touch, but things to smell, because he knows that this is the most evocative by far of our five senses.

And so it was in the sad days of the Highland Clearances that the evicted families took with them and remembered all their lives the smell of peat reek.

As with the drovers, the food in the shielings was almost entirely oatmeal porridge and milk – in this case often sheep's milk, but there was one other essential ingredient in the nourishment of the Highlander which had to be provided – whisky. This was distilled in the most remote corries of the Cairnwell and the Glas Maol, well away from the inquisitive eyes of the gaugers, and I know where there is the remains of one such still in the upper reaches of Glen Taitneach.

The produce of these illegal but important operations was carried down the Glen in small casks or cogies, each holding about five gallons, slung on the backs of ponies. Of necessity, the main road had to be avoided, and the route taken was through the valley called Glacklochan which ends beside the Tomb and extends northwards to Cronaherie. The Reverend Allan Stewart, who was Minister of the Parish at the end of the eighteenth century, on one of his visits to Cronaherie was told that the smugglers had passed by and left a cogie there, and he immediately proceeded to unbutton his waistcoat and open his shirt collar. It was his custom, apparently, on such occasions to give a toast in Gaelic to this effect:

> The Minister of the Parish,
> The Dominie of Kirkmichael,
> Robbie Petrie the Fiddler, for ever! Amen!'

An old man, Donald Ferguson, who died in the 1920s, remembered seeing the ponies with their cogies pass down the Glen. He had had a taste of their contents which he described as 'Verra Fine'.

Long ago, funerals in the Glen required generous supplies of home-made refreshment of this kind. In those days mourners carried the coffin on staves in relays of eight, and as sometimes long distances had to be covered, from time to time the bearers were relieved and fell to the rear where there was a vehicle following with all that was necessary. When a friend who wished to give a little monetary assistance towards the expenses of a funeral asked what was appropriate the prompt reply was 'Twa Gallons.'

On these long marches, a strict etiquette had to be observed that none but the inhabitants of the district through which the funeral passed were allowed to act as bearers, and at the Parish boundary the charge was handed over. However, on the Cairnwell there is a stretch of land of some two hundred yards where the ownership is claimed by both Perthshire and Aberdeenshire, and rivalry over this has always persisted between the men of Braemar and those of Glenshee. On one occasion, as a funeral was passing over the Cairnwell, this rivalry resulted in such a fierce struggle that the coffin was thrown to the ground and burst open, quickly cooling the anger of the mourners. On another occasion it is said that a stalwart Braemar man was heard to call out to an approaching party of bearers, 'If you venture to cross the boundary you will bring one corpse over, but I warrant that you will carry four back!'

Such fierce rivalries have long since given way to more peaceful trials of strength and skill in the Games which take place every autumn in Kirmichael, Glenisla and Braemar. The last is, of course, the most famous Gathering in Scotland and is always attended by members of the Royal Family, but few, I think, know of its origin many hundreds of years ago. Here is the story as handed down for generations in Braemar:

Long, long ago the men of the Braes o' Mar were mighty men. The flower of our days are children to the heroes of those times. They speak of the mettle, the sinews and breath of the present generation. What are they to those of the days of old? M'Gregor of Ballochbuie's oldest son left home in the morning after a boar. He pursued him through Glen Callater, Glen Cluny and the Baddoch, over the hills through Glen Ey – by Carn Vaich, through the Conie and Christie, down Coire-a-Bhrothan, across the Bainock – over the hills and through Glen Ceaully – over the hills and up by Ben Vrotan, Cairntoul and Ben Muicduie – through the Glen Luibeg and the Derry – over the hills through Glen Cuaich, past Ben-na-bord, through Glen Candlic over the Ballochdearg and drove him down to the Dee at Polmanuire, a little above Balmoral.

'Did you see,' asked he at a man working nearby, 'a wild boar pass this way a little ago?'

'You yourself,' replied the man, looking at the wild appearance of the excited M'Gregor, 'are the wildest boar I am likely ever to see.'

'You speak truth,' replied the fiery hunter, driving his spear through him in revenge for his insulting language.

They were in no wise particular in those days.

A little further on he came up with the now exhausted boar, and served him as he had the workman. As the sun was disappearing, he reached his father's door, bearing his prize on his shoulders. This was something, and yet not the best of what the mettle of the times gone by could achieve. Need I speak of another feat? Yes, let it be so.

Malcolm of the Big Head* got another queer idea into it. Next year, when he came to Braemar, he must needs prove the speed and endurance of a vigorous young Celt. His notion was to establish a post system for the kingdom, and this he meant to do by means of foot- runners. All his ten- ants and subjects of Braemar were therefore assembled on the mound of the plain whereon the present castle is built. A splendid baldric and sword, besides a purse of gold, was to be given to the youth who should first reach the summit of Craig Choinnich, as seen from the rendezvous. Among the assembled competitors stood conspicuous the two eldest sons of M'Gregor of Ballochbuie. The runners were ranged. The king held the glass ready to be turned. Three lord judges waved the flag on the hill to signify they were ready. The king struck the shield; the trumpet sounded; the tartans streamed and whistled in the wind; the ground trembled beneath their tramp; the

---

* *Malcolm Canmore (Ceann Mhor), son of King Duncan, murdered by Macbeth in 1039.*

eye seemed to carry them forward, not to follow them; they rose and fell again, bounding like the motion of the swift sea. Just as they reached the foot of the hill, another young man, perspiring profusely, scarlet with heat, breathless with haste, broke into the circle where the king stood viewing the competitors.

'Oh! will you let me run,' cried the youth, 'will you let me run?'

'You are too late, my good fellow,' observed the king.

'Oh! no, no, let me run, let me run;' and unbuckling as he spoke, he had already thrown aside his sword, dirk and skian, tightened the belt of his kilt, and now stood leaning forward on one foot, looking imploringly at the king, and casting every moment an unquiet glance at the racers who were now toiling up the hillside.

'Go if you wish,' said the king; 'but you are too late.'

The youth did not wait to answer.

'Who is he?' enquired Malcolm of his forester.

'The youngest of M'Gregor of Ballochbuie's sons. His two brothers are among those that compete.' The youth cleared the plain, fleet as the stag. The foremost were hanging on the face of the hill above him, diminished to children, and seeming scarcely to move.

Young M'Gregor appeared to leap up like the vigorous goat, now climbing on all fours, now seizing the long heather with his hands and drawing himself up, always up. He stopped no breathing space; he looked not behind; he missed never a step or hold. He reached the last of the line of white that marked the progress of the runners through the long heather and scattered bushes.

'The springal will beat them all,' exclaimed Malcolm; 'look how he ascends!'

'More power to him,' exclaimed our huge old friend Allan Durward, looking as if he meant it.

The race became more and more exciting. Some of the hindermost had indeed given over; but all those who were not despairingly far behind put forth thew and sinew, and pressed close after each other, ready to take advantage of every accident. The two M'Gregors had indeed left the others considerably behind but they might both fail; now was the critical moment. Young M'Gregor sprang forward with unabated energy, passing the others, one after one. They were now hanging on the brow of that steep which

Ling

stands as a wall to a kind of steppe sloping from the east westwards, and from behind which rises the last elevation seen from the plain. The youth was now next to his brothers. They had scaled the steep, but as the last of them was disappearing behind it, his form rose erect on its edge, then bent forward, and plunged in headlong pursuit after them. Now close behind them he cried out,

'Halves, brothers, and I'll stop.'

'Gain what you can,' replied the hero of the boar-hunt, 'and keep what you gain. I will do the same.'

The second was too breathless to speak. The young lad never halted; even while he spoke he rushed onwards, and the first, who had taken a breathing space, saw him pass the second and bound within a few paces of the place where he himself was. They were now engaged on the last steep, and as they re-appeared to the spectators, there were two abreast, both equally ardent, both exerting themselves to the utmost.

'Now, brother,' said the youngest again, 'halves and I will yield.'

'No, never,' returned he, 'keep what you gain.'

They felt their heads dizzy, their eyes dim and painful – the breath rolled quick through their nostrils like fire – their hearts beat louder than their footsteps – every muscle and sinew was tightened to breaking – the foam in their mouths seemed dried into sand – their bleeding lips when closed glued themselves together – the sweat pearled on their skin in cold drops – and their feet rose and fell mechanically more than otherwise. Now they come in sight of the goal – now the judges encourage them by their cheers – now they seem renewed again in vigour. The youngest put his whole soul forth; the oldest summoned up all the strength of his tougher frame. Terribly pressed, he was yet determined to gain, and stretched out his arm to impede the motion of his rival, but felt nothing. They had only four yards to go. He looked to his side, expecting to see him on the ground. At that moment the tartans grazed the skin of his knee. His brother had leapt forward below his outstretched arm. Furious, he bounded on and fell, his hand clutching with iron grasp the kilt of his rival. The youngest was yet two yards from the flag and his strength was exhausted. He could not drag the other's prostrate body one step, and now he saw the hindermost fast approaching, encouraged by the incident. Quick as thought, loosening the belt of his kilt, he resigned it to the hero of the boar hunt.

'I have yielded everything to you hitherto,' quoth he, 'and I will that also.'

He reached the signal with three feeble springs, seized the staff and threw it into the air; then, falling down, buried his face in the fresh heather and damp earth. A loud shout from the plain told that the spectators had seen someone gain. But the victor and his vanquished brothers heard it not. They lay all three, within a few paces of each other, unable to move arm or limb, but they panted so strongly that their bodies seemed to rise of themselves from the ground. When they rose up their faces were deadly pale, chequered with livid black lines and spots. The youngest had reached the top in three minutes.

Thus the origin of the Braemar Games attaches itself to the days of Malcolm of the Big Head.

Eight hundred years later this hill race was still the principal feature of the Braemar Gathering, and was watched with great delight and satisfaction by Queen Victoria, who wrote in her journal:

September 12th 1850

We lunched early, and then went at half-past two o'clock, with the children and all our party, except Lady Douro, to the Gathering at the Castle of Braemar, as we did last year ... There were the usual games of 'putting the stone', 'throwing the hammer' and 'caber', and racing up the hill of Craig Cheunnich, which was accomplished in less than six minutes and a half; and we were all much pleased to see our gillie Duncan, who is an active, good-looking young man, win. He was far before the others the whole way. It is a fearful exertion. Mr Farquharson brought him up to me afterwards. Eighteen or nineteen started, and it looked very pretty to see them run off in their different coloured kilts, with their white shirts (the jackets or doublets they take off for the games), and scramble up through the wood, emerging gradually at the end of it, and climbing the hill.

Little, it seems, had changed in the intervening centuries, except the time taken to reach the summit. But then, did I not just say that long, long ago the men of the Braes o' Mar were mighty men, and the flower of our days are children to the heroes of those times?

6 Diarmid and the Boar

Diarmid's Grave

The story is told to us in an ancient Gaelic poem entitled 'The Death of Diarmid'. It is not to be found in Macpherson's translation of the works of Ossian, but as it deals with the same period about which he writes, and as the main characters are all Fingalian, it is more than possible that it comes from his pen. It tells of the illicit love of Queen Grainne, wife of Fingal the Great, for his brave and handsome nephew Diarmid, and how this ended in the death of both lovers.

It starts thus:

> Hearken a little, I sing you a song
> Of the great and the good who are gone;
> Of Grainne and Finn the triumphant
> And the woeful fate of Macdoon.
>
> Sweet is Glenshee and the valley beside it
> With the voice of elk and deer
> And pleasant its stream tinged so often
> With blood from the Fenian spear.

It seems that the first time Grainne set eyes on Diarmid he was quelling a fight between infuriated dogs. She was captivated by his courage and manly bearing and fell deeply in love with him, so deeply in fact that she managed to persuade him, against his will, to elope with her, swearing she would die if he were to refuse.

Eventually, they returned to the King's court, but Fingal was consumed with rage and jealousy and plotted for Diarmid's death. He invited his nephew to slay a wild boar of enormous size and ferocity which was the terror of the district, and which had its lair in a rocky ravine at the foot of Bengulbein. Fearing that this request was a device to cause the death of her lover, Grainne tried to persuade him not to undertake the task.

> 'O Diarmid! My own one!' said Grainne,
> 'Let the dogs drive the chase o'er the lea.
> Come thou not near the proud son of Cumhal
> Who is wrath with my hero for me.'

Diarmid, however, was too proud to refuse the task of delivering the people of Glenshee from the savage creature. He set off in pursuit and, finding the boar on Bengulbein, he endeavoured to slay it with his spear. The boar, however, seized the spear in its enormous teeth and in a moment chewed it to pieces. Diarmid was undaunted and resumed the attack with his sword. This time he was successful and returned in triumph to the court. The King, who had hoped for and expected quite a different outcome to the encounter, then resorted to a cunning trick. He commanded Diarmid to measure, with his bare foot, the length of his quarry from snout to tail, and then the reverse way, from tail to snout.

As the King had expected, some of the foul, poisoned bristles from the boar's back entered Diarmid's foot. He was dying from the poison, but there was still a chance of recovery if he could obtain a draught from the King's cup, or shell. He begged for this favour, reminding Fingal of the many services he had done him in the past. But the King was implacable, and threw his cup into the lochan at the foot of Bengulbein, where it still lies.

> 'Shall I bring thee a draught, thou fair hero
> From the lake with my life-giving shell
> When the ill in one hour thou hast done me
> Outweighs all the good thou canst tell?'

Diarmid died in agony and Grainne, inconsolable and distracted by grief, flung herself on an arrow and died beside him. Amid the laments of the people they were laid to rest together at the foot of Bengulbein, and a group of large boulders there is said to mark their grave.

> Beneath thy grey stones, O Ben Gulbein,
> The brown-haired chief is laid.
> His blue eyes are sleeping for ever
> Under thy green grassy shade.

It is true that there are other places in Scotland which are given as the scene of the tragedy, but none of these has so many landmarks connected with the poem as Glenshee, and it seems beyond doubt that this is where the death of Diarmid took place.

First, there is Ben Gulbein, referred to in the poem as Ben Goolbein; then on the south side of this mountain there is a steep rugged gulley known as the boar's bed. A mile and a half up Glenbeg and twenty yards to the right of the road is Fingal's Well – Tober-na-Feinne – sometimes known as the Wishing Well, because by walking round it three times holding a cup of water you can obtain your dearest wish. Opposite this, on the other side of the road, is Ossian's Well – Tober-na-Ossian.

On rising ground across the river from the Old Spital Farm is a small lochan into which it is said the King threw his cup, and a little to the south of this is the group of stones which marks the resting place of Queen Grainne, Diarmid and his white hounds.

Some of the names I have mentioned appear in deeds of ownership and transfers of land going back for hundreds of years, and in a Gaelic poem 'The Boar Hunt' written by Allan M'Rory in 1512, the author lays the scene in Glenshee:

Glenshee, the vale that close beside me lies,
Where sweetest sounds are heard of elk and deer
And where the Fein did oft pursue the chase
Following the hounds along the lengthening vale
Below the great Ben Gulbin's grassy height
Of fairest knolls that lie beneath the sun,
The valley winds.

What I have told you has been known and accepted for at least five hundred years, but before we leave the story of Diarmid it is interesting to record that the Clan Campbell trace their lineage to Diarmid, and in their records they are sometimes known as Siol Diarmid, the descendants of Diarmid, son of Duibhane. Their crest is, not surprisingly, a Boar's Head.

Glenshee from Diarmid's Grave. Mount Blair in the distance

7 Raids of the Caterans

The Highlander, the true Highlander, not the industrious Lowland Scot, is a *ceithern* who would rather fight than work, and for this reason, among others, cattle stealing was, for centuries, a way of life in the northern hills.

The lands of Badenoch, Rannoch and Lochaber are poor and bleak, and it was easier (and more exciting) to steal cattle from the fertile glens to the south than it was to rear them at home.

It is recorded in 'Pitcairn's Trials' that in 1591 'The Earl of Ergyle was charged on complaint of Lord Ogilvie of Airlie to appear before King and Privy Council on 28th October for raiding Glen Elay (Isla) on 21st August last, when they murthorit all the inhabitants they could lay hands on, to the nowmor of XVIII or XX, and took much spulzie, including a great nowmor of nolt, schiep, etc. None of the accused appeared on the day appointed and they were pronounced rebels'.

I do not suppose they were in the least concerned about this, for apprehending them would have been nigh impossible and certainly there was no disgrace in being a cateran – very much the reverse – it was considered to be a brave and glorious occupation, and often profitable as well. According to an old rhyme,

> To toom a fauld* or sweep a glen
> Are just the deeds of pretty men

Glenshee and Glenisla were noted for their cattle and were constantly raided by thieving bands who came by way of Glen Tilt to Glenlochsie, then by the back of Bengulbein to the Rhidorrach in Glenbeg, and then over into Glenbrighty and Glenisla. So often did they come by this route that it came to be known as

* *Toom a fauld: Empty a fold.*

the Cateran's Road.

One of the most famous of the Lochaber caterans was Donald Mor Campbell who, until his marriage, was a quiet peaceable man who declined to take part in any of these raids. Marriage, however, changed all this; his wife became envious of all the 'spulzie' brought home by more adventurous men and taunted him so bitterly with his lack of courage and enterprise that one day he felt compelled to set out with a band of his neighbours to 'toom a fauld'. Evidently this was successful, and he must have enjoyed it as well, for he became the leader of all the caterans from Lochaber and a terror to Glenshee, Glenisla, Glenprosen and Glenclunie.

After a long and successful career (which I hope satisfied his wife), he set out with a small band of followers at about the time of the harvest in 1665 and swept the whole of Glencluny. He was pursued by such a large force that his men were inclined to leave the cattle and save themselves, but this was not Donald's way. He told his men to keep together and drive the cattle on as fast as possible, while he would guard the rear against surprise. He then sent his piper off in another direction to mislead the pursuers, and this little ruse succeeded beyond all his hopes. It was now early morning, and as the sun rose the Glencluny men could hear, away on their left, the 'Pibroch of Donald Dubh'. They hastened towards it, but it became gradually fainter and led them south-east towards Glenshee. The piper had had orders to play for a short time in one place and then, keeping hidden by the uneven ground, run on and do the same again. In this way he led the pursuit right down into Glenshee, and when the Glencluny men at last discovered how they had been tricked their fury knew no bounds. The people of Glenshee handed the piper over to them, and when he refused to say which way his countrymen had gone he was shot.

Donald Mor escaped to Lochaber where the sad news soon reached him. He vowed vengeance on the people of Glenshee for what he considered to be their treachery, and planned an immediate raid as punishment. However, most of his usual followers considered they had stirred up such a hornet's nest in the southern Glens that they were unwilling to go with him,

He was not discouraged and set out with only eight men, and such was his skill that even with this small band he managed to lift a large creach from Glenisla and Glenshee. They started on the homeward journey by the usual route, Glenbrighty, over the southern shoulder of Craigleach and up the back of Bengulbein by Alt-na-Duich, the Thieves Burn. This took them into Corrie Shith, but here a thick mist came down and filled the corrie. It was now morning and getting light, but visibility was only a few yards and Donald considered it was safe to light a fire and prepare breakfast. What he did not know was that the men of Glenshee and Glenisla, for once in accord, were close behind him. Some, it is true, fearing an ambush, had turned back, but a small resolute party, with the Glenisla men at their head, pressed on. They were rewarded by seeing the glow of the caterans' fire and three of the Ogilvies crept cautiously forward. Three shadowy forms were seen round the fire and each chose one and fired. Two fell and the third, with his companions and a few cattle, fled up Glenlochsie. Examination of the fallen men revealed that one was Donald Mor himself.

The scene was described to me in all its detail by Alec Lamont of Slochnacraig, who had heard it from Mrs Robertson of Slochnacraig, who had heard it from her father, tenant in Cuthills in the middle of the eighteenth century. That the caterans were indeed having breakfast was clear from Alec's graphic description of Donald's last moment.

'Ogilvie's ball struck him in the back o' the heid and the bread and cheese came fleein' oot o' his mouth as he fell.'

Donald Mor Campbell was agreed by all to have been a brave leader and a handsome man. His plaid and kilt were of one piece, twelve yards long* and there were three dozen silver buttons on his coat – a precaution taken so that, if killed, there would be enough money to pay for a Christian burial.

Although it was usual in those days for cattle thieves to be buried where they fell, such was Donald's reputation that his family and friends from Lochaber sent a request that he should be buried in Glenshee Churchyard. This was agreed, and the expenses were paid by 'Little Eppie', wife of the landlord of the Spital

---

* *The ancient kilted plaid or* breacan feile *worn at this time was a remarkable garment, as was the method of putting it on. It consisted of seven to twelve yards of tartan cloth, sewn up the middle to form a plaid of double width, from four to six yards long by two yards wide. A portion of this length was laid on the ground with the belt under it, the lower and middle portion being then plaited to form a kilt, leaving a flap on either side. The Highlander then lay down upon this, crossed the right flap and next placed the left flap over it and then buckled his belt. When he got up, the upper part of the plaid, which formed a sort of double kilt, was fastened with a brooch on the left shoulder, and part of the plaid on the right side was buckled under the belt. It was not until early in the eighteenth century that the* philabeg *or short kilt emerged as a separate garment. (From a lecture given to the Scottish Society in 1920 by Mr Loudon Macqueen Douglas.)*

Inn, who repaid herself by selling his buttons to Ramsay of Cronaherie. These were afterwards worn by his son the *Duine* who came to be known as 'Puton Aragid'.

To mark the spot where Donald fell his comrades erected a cairn at the foot of Corrie Shith. It is somewhat overgrown now but can easily be seen by those who know where to look.

It is said that Ogilvie of Holt who slew him was so afraid of revenge that he always went about armed, and even when at home sat facing the door with a gun close at hand, but no-one ever ventured to harm him.

The other well-known cateran's rhyme which we were taught as children reads:

> The mountain sheep are sweeter,
> But the valley sheep are fatter.
> We therefore deemed it meeter
> To carry off the latter.

The uniform of the Black Watch in 1746.

8 M'Comie Mor

M'Comie Mor was descended from a branch of Clan M'lntosh, and we know that his family had been established in Glenshee for many years. In the Roll of the broken clans in the Highlands and Isles, in the Act of Parliament 'for punishment of thift, reiff, oppression and soirning' of 1594, there are included, under 'many brokin men', 'M'Thomas in Glensche and Ferquharsonis in Bra of Mar'.

'Brokin men' in this context merely meaning those that belonged to septs which had broken away from the main clan or family.

M'Comie was a man of intrepid bravery and enormous physical strength. He was also the finest swordsman of his time, and these three attributes combined to make him a hero in his own time and a legend still in Glenshee and Glenisla.

When a young man he had the good fortune to be instructed in the art of swordsmanship by a famous master of the art. He was an apt pupil and when he was about to leave his instructor said:

'You are now a perfect master of your weapon, save for one thing.'

'What is that?' said M'Comie.

'It is the drawing of your sword and placing yourself on guard in one swift motion. If suddenly attacked, you might be killed before you were ready with your defence.'

He was duly instructed in this important part of the swordsman's art, and to the end of his life he continued to draw his sword with a peculiarly graceful sweep which, on at least one occasion, saved his life.

Of the many stories about him the best known, perhaps, concerns the Clach-na-Coileach, the scene of one of those acts of chivalry and courage which were so characteristic of him.

The 'Cockstone'

In the sixteenth and seventeenth centuries, the proprietors in Glenshee held
their land in feu charter from the Earls of Athole who were entitled to levy kain,
or fowls, from every house with a 'reeking chimney'. This annual levy had all
gone well one year from the head of the Glen down to a little cot at Cnoc-Liath,
just above Finegand. Here the kain gatherers found a poor widow woman, a
tenant of M'Comie, and, no doubt thinking her an easy victim unable to defend
her property, they seized, not just their rightful due, but every fowl she possessed. Tears and entreaties were of no avail and the poor old woman was in
despair. There was only one man who could help her, and she hurried down to
Finegand with her sad story and begged M'Comie for help. To her great joy he
at once agreed to her request and, as the kain gatherers were by now well down
the Glen, they set off with all speed, the widow no doubt recounting, as she
hurried by his side, details of the harsh and greedy conduct of the earl's men.
At last they came up with these villains beside the great stone, where M'Comie
explained to them the circumstances of the poor widow and asked for the return
of the fowls to which they had no right. This polite request was met with a
rough and rude refusal – after all, they were many and he was only one. The
old woman was again in despair, thinking that this time she had indeed lost her
fowls for good, but M'Comie was furious. To be refused a rightful request was
bad enough, but to be insulted on his own land was more than a proud chieftain
could bear. The civil request to return part of his tenant's property became an
angry demand to return the whole. This again was refused and M' Comie, seeing

that words were useless, resorted to force. He drew his sword and attacked the leader of the earl's men. The man's companions saw his plight and, dropping their creels, rushed to his assistance. They were too late. By the time they reached him, he had paid the price of those who dared to insult M'Comie. (Others had done so before and others would do so again). Now M'Comie was attacked on all sides, but with every blow of his sword an Athole man fell and the remainder, unwilling to share the same fate and seeing more of the Glenshee men approaching, turned and fled down the Glen, leaving the baskets of fowls on the ground where they had dropped them.

M'Comie then strode forward and with his sword cut open the creel containing the widow's fowls, whereupon one young cock flew up onto the stone and sent forth a loud, clear crow of victory and defiance. It is a story known to everyone in the Glen, and whenever I pass the stone I can picture the scene; the proud laird sheathing his sword and by now surrounded by his clansmen; the joyful old woman, and high above them all on top of the stone, the young cock, with bright red comb and burnished feathers, sending out his shrill call of defiance to the retreating Athole men.

However, as might be expected, this was not the end of the matter. The earl could not brook the double insult of having his kain withheld and his men routed by one of his vassals. An armed band was therefore sent from Athole to Glenshee with orders to take M'Comie, dead or alive, to Blair Castle. In due course they arrived at Finegand and surprised the laird unarmed in his house. They explained their errand and M'Comie could see that fight and flight were useless. He admitted that he was powerless to resist them, but pointed out that it was a long journey back to Blair Athole and both he and they would be the better of a meal before they set out. They were all at this time in the kitchen, and M'Comie gave orders for refreshments to be prepared at the other end of the house. While this was being done, he endeavoured to put the Athole men at their ease, and by the time the meal was ready he had been so successful that he was able to persuade them to lay aside their arms and plaids so as to be more comfortable during their meal. As he himself was unarmed and seemed so affable and friendly, they readily agreed to this and the arms and plaids were piled in a corner of the kitchen. All then proceeded to the other end of the house and found a true Highland spread laid out on the table. They ate heartily, and under the influence of this generous hospitality and a liberal supply of *uisge-beatha* they became even more relaxed and at ease.

M'Comie then begged to be excused for a short time as he had to give instructions for the management of his property during his absence. He said he would let them know as soon as he was ready to accompany them. A short time later, one of the servants announced that her master was ready. The Athole men then returned to the kitchen to resume their arms and plaids, but here the good humour of a few minutes earlier turned to dismay and fear. Before them stood M'Comie, fully armed, while on the table in front of him were their plaids neatly laid out. Of the guns and weapons there was no sign.

M'Comie, no longer the genial host, informed them in a haughty tone that they were now at liberty to take him, but he would defend himself with all his strength. Such was his reputation that the earl's men knew their task was impossible and there was nothing for it but to gather up their plaids and return to Blair Castle without their arms. M'Comie had again come off victorious, but he was in no doubt that the earl, smarting under this double insult, would redouble his efforts to take him, and this would certainly have happened in the end but for an unforseen event.

A professional swordsman had just arrived at Blair Castle. He was a gigantic Italian, and on his arrival he had issued a challenge to the best man the earl could produce from all his vast estates. If the earl could not produce a man, or if he did and that man were defeated, the Italian would claim a sum of money, and such were his size and ferocious aspect, as well as his reputation as a swordsman, that no man could be found in Athole to accept his challenge. This was a source of much distress to the earl. The money meant nothing to him, but his reputation was at stake and he was facing humiliation at the hands of this foreign bully if not one of his subjects could be found to match him. In this emergency his thoughts turned to M'Comie. Recent events bore testimony to his courage, strength and skill and the earl was prepared to forgive his past acts of defiance if he would come to Blair Castle and restore the reputation of Athole. And so a trusted servant was despatched to Finegand with the message that, if M'Comie would return with him to Blair Castle and render a personal service to the earl, the past would be forgiven. At first, M'Comie suspected that this was just a trick to get him to Blair Castle where retribution for his past deeds would surely follow, but in the end he was persuaded of the earl's good intentions and he set out with the messenger. However, on arrival at Blair Castle another difficulty arose. When confronted with the Italian champion and told the reason why he had been summoned, he flatly refused to fight a man with whom, as he said, he had no quarrel. The hopes of the Athole men which had been raised so high by the accounts of the kain gatherers and by M'Comie's magnificent personal appearance were again dashed.

The earl urged and entreated him, but to no avail, and whispers began that the mighty M'Comie might not be such a brave man after all. The Italian then, putting M'Comie's reluctance down to cowardice, began to taunt him, and when this had no effect on the imperturbable Highlander, he resorted to a physical insult. Walking round behind M'Comie, he lifted the chieftain's kilt with one hand and gave him a resounding smack on his bare buttocks with the flat of his sword.

In an instant, with that beautiful, graceful sweep which was peculiar to him, M'Comie drew his sword and put himself on guard. The Italian sprang back and did the same. Now a breathless hush fell on the hall of Blair Castle as the two huge opponents faced each other, for those watching could see that on M'Comie's face which meant that this was indeed a fight to the death. They had not long to wait. After a few preliminary parries, and with a speed the eye could scarcely follow, M'Comie's blade was through the Italian's guard and the insult was avenged.

Cock Salmon

But it was not just by mortal men that M'Comie's strength was tested. In those days magic and supernatural forces were more often met with than they are today, and M'Comie had at least two encounters with water kelpies which tested not only his strength, but his wits as well. The first of these took place when he was living at Finegand. The house then, as now, was only a few yards from the river Shee, and one evening, as M'Comie was taking a last look around before going to bed, he heard loud despairing cries coming from the river,

'M'Comie Mor! Help! Help me! M'Comie Mor!'

At this time the river was in flood and over its banks, and M'Comie had no doubt that someone attempting the ford just above Finegand had been swept away and was drowning. Seizing a long staff, he rushed to the swollen river and started wading towards the bank, giving encouraging shouts to whoever it was in the water to let that unfortunate person know that help was at hand. It was now getting dark, but he saw what he thought was a man's head, and to his relief it seemed that the current would take it within reach of his staff. Steadying himself as the object approached, he saw an arm come out of the water and make a desperate clutch at the end of the staff; but instead of feeling the body coming towards him, he felt a tremendous pull on the staff which would have dragged an ordinary man into the flooded river. At once he knew that he was not dealing with a drowning man, but with the water kelpie himself. He was furious with this treacherous attempt to drown him, and in his turn gave a tremendous pull on the staff which almost landed the kelpie on dry land. The kelpie, equally furious that he had met his match, gave a scream of rage and let go the staff which M'Comie aimed at his head as he disappeared in the darkness.

Although I lived at Finegand for many years and have fished on the Spey, I have been fortunate that I have never come across the kelpie. I know that from time to time he visits the ford above Finegand and that one of his favourite rivers is the Spey, along whose banks are miles of rich green pastures. Here the unwary walker or fisherman may see quietly grazing a beautiful white pony – but beware! Overcome by the magic beauty of this creature, you will feel an irresistible urge to jump onto its back. Once there you are lost. With a neigh of delight it will gallop off and carry you into the river. It is not a beautiful white pony at all, but the kelpie in his favourite disguise, and he will drown you if he can.

M'Comie's next adventure was with the kelpie's wife. It was after he went to live at Crandart in Glenisla. One day, as he went through the forest of Canlochan, he came upon this creature in the weird and secluded Glascorrie. Taken by surprise, she had no chance to escape to the water before M'Comie had seized her; but how was he to get her to Crandart? He knew that if he crossed running water with her she would escape, and this meant a long and tortuous journey round the headwaters of all the streams, along the summits of Craig Lecach, Cairn Aighe, Black Hill and Monamenach, but at last he arrived at Crandart. Here his captive had to bargain for her release, and it was agreed that she would secure her freedom if she would give M'Comie some information concerning the manner of his death. Taking him to the window, she pointed to a large conspicuous stone on the hillside.

'You will die with that stone under your head,' she prophesied, and, true to his word, he released her.

The next day he arranged for the stone to be removed from the hillside and built into the wall of the house under the head of his bed. Many years later, the prophesy of the kelpie's wife came true and M'Comie died peacefully with the stone under his head.

Among the many stories of M'Comie's enormous physical strength is the one of how he came to acquire a bull on what were, to him, very easy terms. The animal had apparently become unmanageable and M'Comie had heard the owner say that he would have to destroy it. This seemed ridiculous to M'Comie who laughed at the idea of a man being beaten by a bull. Annoyed at this ridicule, the owner of the bull, Mercer of Meikleour, said,

'Very well, if you can manage this bull by yourself, you can have him as a present.'

The offer was at once accepted and the two men went to the enclosure where the bull was confined. On seeing them, it rushed bellowing to the fence. M'Comie, leaning over, seized the bull's right horn with his left hand and, vaulting over, seized the other horn with his right hand and in a moment had the animal on its back. He then allowed it to get to its feet and threw it again, repeating the process till the bull was completely subdued. He then took it home in triumph.

Since hearing this story, I have sometimes wondered how he would have dealt with the polled Aberdeen Angus cattle his descendants bred so successfully in later years.

The lintel stone, 76″ x 36″ x 7″

Another story of uncanny physical strength concerns one of my own family, Colin M'Kenzie. There can still be seen an enormous granite stone forming the lintel of the lime kiln at Crandart, and how it came there was by the unaided efforts of one man.

M'Comie was universally considered the strongest man in Glenshee and Glenisla, but was he?

Let me tell you the story and you can decide.

He and his stalwart sons were building the kiln and had been struggling all morning to get the stone in place when there appeared this man M'Kenzie, who sat down on a grassy bank a little way off and watched their efforts. When the time came for the mid-day meal, M'Comie, with true Highland hospitality, suggested that M'Kenzie, although he had not offered to help with the work, should join them. M'Kenzie declined and remained seated where he was, while M'Comie and his sons repaired to the house.

On their return, M'Kenzie was still seated on the bank, but the huge stone was now firmly and accurately in place over the doorway of the kiln.

It is said that M'Comie made no comment on this miraculous feat, but simply took off his coat *with its silver buttons* and, without a word, handed it to M'Kenzie. The old chief knew that it had needed more than mortal strength to do what had been done, and thought it wise to propitiate his strange visitor.

The last tale I will tell you about this great man illustrates the family pride which has always been such a marked characteristic of the Highlander.

M'Comie, as he grew older, began to feel his physical strength declining with the passing years. He had several sons, but was a little doubtful about the character of the eldest who, like himself, was called John. This young man, also called Mor on account of his size and strength, had a quiet and peaceable nature and M'Comie thought him too gentle, with, as he said, 'too much of the Campbell blood in him'. This, he thought, was not likely to increase his courage, and one day he decided to put his son to the test.

Meadow Pipit - 'parachute' display.

Knowing that young John would be returning one evening from Glenshee to Glenisla by the pass of Bainie, he lay in wait for him by a sort of stone seat still known as M'Comie's Chair. He disguised himself as well as he could and trusted to the failing light to conceal his identity. When his son appeared, he sprang up and, without a word of warning, attacked him. John, however, recognised him immediately by the graceful sweep with which he drew his sword and guessed the real reason for the attack. Concealing his suspicions, he defended himself with all his might, while demanding the reason for the attack.

Receiving no answer, he continued the fight with such strength and skill that in the end he disarmed his attacker. He then told his exhausted and, for the first time in his life, defeated assailant that if he wished to save his life he must reveal himself. On hearing his father's voice, he reproached him bitterly, saying that he could have killed him several times in the fight and would have done so had he not recognised him at the outset by the way he drew his sword and began the attack. He pointed out what a dreadful thing it would have been had either killed the other, but the old laird replied contentedly that that was no matter; he now had proof of his son's courage and skill and knew that he was a true M'Comie.

As well as his adventures in his native glens, M'Comie braved many dangers with his friend James Graham, Marquis of Montrose, and gave that great man shelter at Finegand when hard pressed by the Covenanting armies; but these events do not concern us here.

His death on 12th January 1676 was greeted with great rejoicing by the caterans of the north and west, and we have two accounts of how they received the news. The first tells how one of them, on returning from the south, joyously exclaimed in answer to the question, '*Ciod an sgeul?*' ('What news?')

'*Sgeul, agus deagh sgeul! Beannaichte gu robh an Oighe Muire! cha bheo MacOmie Mor am braigh na macharach, ge'd bu mhor agus bu laidir e!*' ('News, and good news! Blessed be the Virgin Mary! The great M'Comie in the head of the Lowlands is dead, for as big and strong as he was!')

Another even more graphic account comes from Major Chalmers, a descendant of the Ramsays of Glenbeg:

> When M'Comie Mor died, the caterans greatly rejoiced. So eager were they to communicate the glad tidings to each other, that many of them went to friends' houses at a great distance that night, rapped on the window and said in Gaelic,
>
> 'We have news for you. M'Comie Mor of the mouth of the Lowlands is dead.' They replied,
>
> 'We are very glad to hear it. We will now not be afraid to make our forays, and take the moon at its height.'

John M'Intosh, M'Comie Mor, was, and still is, a legend, and it was a sad day when, three hundred and fifty years ago, his family left Glenshee for ever.

To end this chapter here is the story of another Scottish swordsman, Donald Farquharson of Monaltrie. He was not a native of Glenshee but is included here because he was a contemporary and cousin of M'Comie, both being descended from the great Finla Mor of a hundred years earlier. Like M'Comie, he faced an

Italian, but Monaltrie's victory was the more remarkable, for in his case he had challenged a mysterious and deadly opponent who had made a pact with the Devil and was shielded from all harm by his evil associate. I give you the story as it was told two hundred years ago to John Grant 'in the free and ready language in which he heard it by the fireside in Mar'.

On Monday, 19th October 1640, Skipper Findlay embarked within his ship the Lord Ogilvie, the lairds of Pitfoddels, elder and younger, the young laird of Drum, Donald Farquharson of Tilliegarmonth, Mr James Sibbald, minister at Aberdeen, and to the sea for England go they.

Soon an Italian came to London, a wonderful man, a wizard, a magician, a necromancer, having communion with the Prince of Darkness, and he 'cropped the causey', and none durst impede; and he challenged the bravest cavalier in the kingdom to combat – and he slew all those that came forth against him – and he lived like a prince magnificently – and the burden of his living fell upon the city – and it was grieved greatly – and the laws of chivalry were, that he might so live until vanquished by the champion of the challenged city – and the city offered a measure of gold to the man who would do its battle successfully – and no man could be found – and the king was troubled exceedingly for the burden weighing on his good subjects – and the stranger passed daily before his palace proudly – and a drummer preceded him, inviting some gallant knight to the ordeal – and the cavaliers of the court hung down their heads – and many a lady clothed in black shuddered at the sound – and the daughter of Henry of Navarre lifted up her proud head, and looked sneeringly at the assemblage of goodly knights around her. 'And is there none,' said she, 'in all our realms, for love of king and country, for love of lady fair, or yet for love of me, would draw his sword against this stranger knight of Italy?'

And an eldern lord replied, 'No, there is none, except a certain Scot – Donald Og of Monaltrie.'

And the king said, 'Go, summon him to our presence,' and a messenger was sent.

All were now anxiously awaiting his return with the 'certain Scot', curious and impatient to see him who was presumed to be the first sword in Britain. But, alas! instead of their welcome tread on the stair, the sound of the hateful drum struck on their ears from without, and the challenge sounded clear in the noon-tide air; and nearer it came, and nearer still.

A king's messenger, accompanied by a tall Highlander, met the procession. The challenge was just repeated, and the drum was to beat; but –

'There,' exclaimed Donald Og, thrusting his sword in at one end and out at the other, 'hae done with your din.'

The Italian stepped up before his drummer, demanding who he was that dared presume to offer this insult.

'Sir Stranger, I am Donald Farquharson of Monaltrie and Tilliegarmont, the Chief of *Clann Fhearchar* and ready and willing to meet thee in such wise, and when and where it listeth thee.'

Our hero was no little deal amused to find he had anticipated the queen's wish and the king's request; and no less amazed to hear, for the first time, of the fame and deeds of the southern knight. But the gallant Donald Og only rejoiced the more that he had an opponent worthy of his sword. Brave Donald Og, need we wonder if at thy departure from that 'high hall', the tears sparkled like diamonds in many a bright eye, the deep sigh was heaved by many a fair bosom, and the fond wish, the earnest prayer, preferred by many a lip for thy success?

That evening, Donald, in disguise, repaired to the hotel where the Italian lived. After the master had retired to rest, he made acquaintance in the hall with his servant, a pot, keep-it-up, a rollicking, a brandy-and-wine acquaintance.

'Friend, thou art a man in a hundred,' said the Celt, stretching out his hand to the valet, 'but how art thou employed in this great city?'

'Carissimo,' replied he, working Donald's arm like a pump handle, 'I'm in the great Italian swordsman's service.'

'Indeed! A wonderful man, and invincible, I hear; is it so?'

'As thou sayest, mio caro,' assented the valet, 'but such is the foolishness of the youth of the age, that after slaying whole hecatombs of them, another has again challenged him for tomorrow.'

'Comrade, that youth had well say his *confiteor* tonight. Fill your glass.'

The valet emptied it also.

'My master bears a charmed life; no man of woman born can kill him; no man whose person bears iron can hurt him; no man who treads in leather shoes can prevail against him; no sword that iron ever touched, or leather sheath received, can pierce him; in fine, if the sword be withdrawn from the wound, he revives again; and while fighting he has a shade on each side, which leads his opponent to believe that he has three fighting against him.'

That night, a poor officer's widow made a scabbard of the finest silk knitting, with all gorgeous and quaint devices in raised embroidery, and thenceforth she was rich.

That night, a needy, neglected tailor undid a splendid suit, and made it up again, supplying what lacked after an unusual manner, and from that time customers trooped to his door, and he sported golden angels.

That night, the most fashionable shoemaker made a pair of fine blue velvet slippers, sown over with seed-pearls in the form of a thistle, and strangely soled with the prepared bark of a tree; and he paid a visit to the Old Lady of Threadneedle Street in the morning.

That night, the descendant of the best armourer of Grenada, an exiled Moor, fashioned a sword on a stone anvil with flint hammers, caring greatly that it should touch no iron, and handed it, polished and finished, wrapped up in a linen cloth, to a man who had watched him untiringly from evening till grey dawn; and that Moor spoke of the pilgrimage to Mecca through the day, and of a shop in the Bezestein of Grand Cairo.

Bright and early, Donald Og rose from refreshing sleep, and found in attendance a goodly array of his friends and countrymen. The fashion of his garb struck them not a little; but there were other things to speak of, and it passed uncriticised. The rendezvous gained, the Italian was there, and a throng of the most celebrated persons of the time. If Donald Og's raiment seemed strange to his friends, it did no less so to his antagonist. He felt for the first time in his life alarmed, and tried to touch his adversary's sword with iron, but failed in the attempt.

'When thou touchest my sword, stranger, it shall be in thy body,' exclaimed Donald Og.

They at once engaged, and three opponents appeared before young Monaltrie; but he only heeded the mid one. It was a desperate fight, and the spectators looked on in silence, and their eyes felt sore and dazzled by the rapid flashing of the steel, as it were by lightning. The Italian, though alarmed, felt that his was a charmed life, and at every onset would, with his two shadows, leap shoulder high, and fall on his enemy with dreadful downward plunge. But the Celt parried and thrust undauntedly, and the sharp rattle of the steel grated on the spectators' ears, and their eyes, fascinated by the terrible struggle, stared on unwinkingly. And the combat continued desperate and relentless, the swords jarring together, and the wrists stiffened into iron. Again and again came the dread downward thrust, and again the quick, sure parry, and the Scot's sword glittered through the Italian's side.

'I have it,' said he, 'withdraw thy sword, Scot.'

'Let the spit go with the roast,' replied Donald Og.

'The devil,' groaned the Italian, 'hath kept ill faith with me, or man of woman born should never have overcome me.'

'The devil hath kept good faith with thee, for I was cut out of my mother's side.'

Loud applause rent the sky while these words passed between the combatants, and the Italian fell back and expired. The measure of gold was brought forward and handed to the victor, but some envious, sordid wretches exclaimed, 'See how the Scots beggar pockets our English gold!'

Donald, overhearing this brutal observation, as every other one present did, scattered the gold among the crowd, crying out, 'See how the English dogs gather up the gold which they could not themselves win, but which a Scot won for them!'

The English pocketed the affront with the gold, and Donald Farquharson of Monaltrie was thence styled, 'DomhnulI Og na h-Alba'.

♂ Stonechat - spring.

9 *The Cam Ruadh*

The Cam Ruadh must have been the ugliest little man in all the length and breadth of Scotland three hundred years ago. Just five feet tall, he had, as his name implies, red hair and but one eye. As one man described him long ago:

He had a provoking, warty little nose that came out between his eyes, broad and flat like my thumb, and turned up into the air in a most impertinent pug, just as if it were not worth its pains to smell anything earthly. A pair of broad cheeks whereon you could see every rough, red, knotted vein like the ditches of a cornfield on a dry summer ended on each side of the nose with a hump below the eyes, in a thin crop of red whiskers, the birse of which went away scrambling everywhere, as in a desperate search for their neighbours. I said his eyes – pardon me, he had but one that could be called an eye. In place of the other was a lump of unseemly matter, covered with bluish transparent skin, streaked with blotches of blood and staring wide open. His thin lips seemed to have fasted and dried a year or two in the roost, such a couple of ghost intruments they were; and when determinedly pressed together the strong broad tusks within showed their inequalities through them in a way to make a tender person's flesh creep. Had a tuft of dry rushes, mixed with waterwrack, been substituted for his hair, the crop, to outward appearance, would have been the same. As the head stood then, like a kind of hedgehog, it appeared impossible to make any sense of it. I must, however, I think, make an exception in favour of his seeing eye, a large border of red surrounding a bright circle of blue – so bright indeed that it shone like a star, defying mortal vision to withstand its glance. The frame of the Cam Ruadh, though rather short, was strong as a block of oak, and as to his arms and hands, not Sampson, Gog or Magog rejoiced in better. His legs were shockingly bandied, I grant you, and his feet as flat as shingles. What of that? 'A man's a man for a' that' and the Cam Ruadh was possessed of many enviable qualifications and acquirements. He could have distinguished a bluebottle on a greyish stone at a distance of twenty yards, one-eyed as he was. He could send an arrow twice as far as an ordinary person, with force to kill an ox and accuracy to hit a midge. I am not aware that he considered his bandy legs or flat feet personal beauties; but not hind, hound or hare could beat them at a long race, and but little at a short one. No person could say much of the Cam Ruadh's sentiments, for he seldom said more than three words at a time. As to his character, he was a snappish, crusty, snarling cur who would put up with nobody, as obstinate as a pig and a deal more cunning than a fox, but, such as he was, he found the way of winning one fair damsel's heart and descendants of theirs are still among us.

In his day, Glenshee, where he had his little farm, and the neighbouring glens of Strathardle and Glenisla were constantly being raided by fierce bands of caterans from Badenoch and Lochaber, and the Cam Ruadh had acquired a deadly hatred of these men. It is said that he shot them down like 'houdie craws' till their bodies littered the glens and corries and the air smelled of carrion; but one day, as he came home from the hill, he became disgusted with the sights he met and he made a vow that he would not, for the space of one day, lift his hand against another human, be he cateran or kern, unless in self-defence.

As ill luck would have it, that very night a strong band of caterans swooped down on Glenshee and Glenisla and carried off a large creach of cattle. Both glens were in ferment and the men set off in furious pursuit. It was arranged that the Glenshee men should attack from one side and the Glenisla men from the other, and, to make sure of success, a swift messenger was sent to M'Coinnich Mor na Dalach (Big M'Kenzie of Dalmore) asking him to hasten to their assistance. By morning, all three parties were on the march and the caterans, knowing they would be pursued, had taken up a good defensive position in a hollow on the east side of the Cairnwell, still known as the 'Cateran's Howe'. Unfortunately, in their haste, the men of Glenshee and Glenisla had not chosen a leader, nor had they made a firm rendezvous, and this lack of planning was to have almost fatal results. The Glenshee men arrived first in small straggling bands and, although greatly outnumbered, attacked immediately with more courage than good sense. This unequal fight went on for some three hours and the Glenshee men were hard pressed, while their cowardly neighbours from

Glenisla stationed themselves on the Maol-Odhar and watched to see how the battle would go.

They had their chance to join in when the brawny miller of Glenshee arrived with his seven sons and the strongest party yet of Glenshee men, but still they waited and watched. Meanwhile, the Cam Ruadh, who had come up with the other Glenshee men, could only fret and fume and repent of his oath as he watched his neighbours in their unequal fight. The miller and his sons did prodigies of valour, but one by one the sons fell, and when the miller was told of this he cried, 'We must fight today and lament tomorrow.'

But there was to be no tomorrow for him either. Standing over the last of his sons, he at length sank to his knees. A stout cateran engaged him, but after a few strokes stepped back, knowing that his opponent had only a few moments to live and fearful of the last dying efforts of so formidable a foe. It was now exactly mid-day, and the miller cast one longing look in the direction of Braemar, hoping to see the Mackenzies; but what he saw instead was a slight movement behind a stone on the hillside above him and a piercing blue eye whose light seemed to enter his brain. His strength returned and at the same moment there was a twang and a hiss in the air. The cateran, who had returned and stood with uplifted sword to give his antagonist the *coup de grâce*, gave a terrible cry and leapt in the air. The miller sprang to his feet and the two clasped each other in their arms and, with their dirks driven to the hilt in each others backs, fell dead together.

Now consternation seized the caterans. Arrow after arrow came, they knew not whence, dealing death in their ranks. Every one found its mark till there were eighteen men lying dead in the heather. But then a sudden gust of wind caught the end of the hidden archer's plaid and his hiding place was revealed. With a yell of fury the caterans charged up the hill towards him. The Cam Ruadh fitted the last arrow to his bow, but it snapped and fell useless to the ground. With a curse he hurled the bow after it and leapt from his hiding place. A flight of arrows from the Glenshee men covered his retreat, but he was cut off from them and fled down the hill, leaping juniper bushes, stones and streams like a deer. He out-distanced his pursuers every minute, but the foremost of these bent his bow and sent one last arrow after him. It flew with unerring aim and entered his back, but on he ran. The caterans loosed one last shower of arrows but they all fell short of their mark and the pursuers returned to their comrades, just in time to hear a distant shout and an answering one from the Glenshee men, 'Hurrah! M'Coinnich Mor and the Braemar men!'

At this, the Glenisla men at last came down from the Maol-Odhar, and the caterans, seeing the three parties at last united, took flight, leaving their spoils behind. When the Glenisla men arrived with a thousand excuses, they were greeted by the men of Glenshee and Braemar with fury and scorn and told to take their cattle and be gone. The Braemar men then set off in pursuit of the thieves, but it was a forlorn sight they left behind them, and the remaining Glenshee men went sadly home with their flocks. It was said that next day twenty widows, mostly M'Kenzies, came to collect their dead.

Meanwhile, the poor Cam Ruadh, as he made his way down the glen, was greeted all the way with the comment '*Chaim-Ruaidh, Chaim-Ruaidh! tha saighead na do thoine!*' ('Cam Ruadh, Cam Ruadh! there's an arrow in your back!') to which he testily replied, '*Tha fios agam fhein air sin.*' ('I am well aware of that myself.')

At last he reached home in Glentaitneach, but how to extract the arrow? His wife tugged and pulled, but to no avail, and it was left to the fertile brain of the Cam himself to find the solution. Lying face down on the floor, his wife stood on his back with one foot on either side of the arrow and resumed her efforts. Now she was successful, and out it came, bringing with it a large piece of her unfortunate husband's flesh. As we know, he was a man of few words and he made no comment, but calmly sat down to replace the deficit with a large helping of venison, having first taken from its accustomed place another bow and a quiverful of arrows, in case of an unpleasant interruption to his dinner.

Now it so happened that among those slain by the Cam Ruadh's arrows in the battle on the Cairnwell was the Baron M'Diarmid, a Campbell chieftain from Lochaber. This man had seven sons who soon discovered the identity of the deadly archer, and they made it their business to avenge their father's death. They came looking for the Cam Ruadh and found him one wet and misty day, herding his sheep and cattle. He was wrapped in an old blanket and, dripping wet, he looked a miserable sight, muttering to himself like a fool. Suddenly he felt a tap on his shoulder and, turning round, he knew at once who his visitors were. There was no escape, but he had not been recognised and in a moment he had devised a plan to turn the tables on his adversaries.

'Let us go on,' said one of them, 'there's no use talking to that fool.'

'No matter if he's a fool or no',' said another, 'if he tells us what we want to know.'

'My lad,' said their leader, 'can you show us where the Cam Ruadh lives?'

'Perhaps I can,' said the Cam.

'Is it far from here?'

'Perhaps it is,' replied the Cam with a foolish grin, staring with apparent wonder at their bows and arrows. He could not understand this strange style of walking stick with a string attached to it, and when the owner, thinking to gain his confidence, handed one to him he capered round with it like an idiot.

'Come, my lad,' said the Campbell, 'I'll give you one of these if you tell me where the Cam Ruadh lives.'

'Which one?' said the Cam, looking them over.

'Whichever one you please, and a quiverful of arrows as well, if you tell us where the Cam Ruadh lives.'

'Very well,' said the Cam, 'but what is the use of these things?'

'A good question indeed,' said one of the band, 'show him how to use them, Captain.'

The Cam Ruadh opened his mouth in wonder when the leader fitted an arrow to his bow and sent it flying over the stream. He seized a bow and emptied a pile of arrows onto the ground beside him. Then he held the bow the wrong way round and, putting an arrow to the string, he pointed it at his own breast. The laughter of the band grew louder at every antic, but at last he managed to shoot some arrows over the stream, running excitedly after each one as he did so. In the end, getting tired of this, he shot the entire quiverful over the stream, some going in one direction and some in another, till he had only one left. At that moment, a bird alighted on the stone which had been chosen as a mark. The Cam's one eye lit up like a fire, the last arrow flew on its way and the bird fell dead.

'A splendid shot!' cried the Cam as he bounded over the stream with the bow in his hand to gather up his victim. This he did, waving it round his head and shouting all the time, 'Splendid! Splendid!'

The Campbells, of course, thought this was a pure chance shot and allowed him to gather up the rest of the arrows. Then, having done this, and holding the dead bird with the arrow through it in one hand and the bow with an arrow fitted to the string in the other, the Cam stepped behind a large stone and cried out, 'I am the Cam Ruadh!'

He then bent down behind the stone and all the band of Campbells could see was the tip of an arrow pointing straight at them.

'Mercy,' called their chief, 'and we'll retire without harm to anyone.'

'If you don't ... ,' replied the Cam, and he drew the bow to its full stretch.

But his enemies waited no longer – they turned and ran, with the Cam following in their rear and encouraging the flight with wild shouts of derision. At last they were out of sight and, convinced they would not return, at least for the present, he returned to his flocks.

However, he had not been forgotten and the seven brothers, humiliated by their last encounter with him, were more determined than ever to exact their revenge.

Next winter, they set out again to find him, but before they could reach his house they were overtaken by one of those winter storms which those who do not know the Highland glens cannot imagine. The drifts got deeper and deeper and the howling wind drove the frozen snow into their faces like a shower of needles.

Meanwhile, the Cam and his wife sat by the fireside in their home – modest as it was, with one end devoted to barn, byre and stable and the other to kitchen and bedroom. The windows were closed by shutters instead of glass and there was a little pantry leading off the kitchen. Here the Cam, on such a night, thought himself very comfortable indeed, and as he sat by the fireside with his wife she said to him, 'What would you do, Cam, if the caterans came tonight?'

'Give them meat,' he replied.

'And then?' continued his wife.

'Let them sleep,' said the Cam.

'And at last?' persisted his wife, astonished at his unaccustomed moderation.

'Let them be gone,' he answered.

'Be as good as your word,' said a voice from outside, 'for we were never more in need of what you promise.'

The Cam, who little expected visitors on such a night, was armed in a moment, but called out, 'Surrender your arms first.'

'Send out your wife then, Cam Ruadh, and we will give up our arms to her.'

The arms were safely stored in the pantry and the brothers were allowed in to thaw their frozen limbs by the fire. A sheep was brought in from the fold to satisfy their hunger, and was washed down with a cogie of good ale. Peace and goodwill were established, and when the Campbells left next morning an alliance, both offensive and defensive, was agreed upon. They were all now the best possible friends.

Some time after this, the sept to which the seven brothers belonged came into open conflict with another clan and, according to the alliance, the Cam was sent for. He set out at once, but arrived just too late – the brothers had left and only their mother greeted him.

'Are you going to help them?' she asked, looking with disbelief at this extraordinary little man. He did not look in the least like a *ceithern* or fighting man.

'Yes,' he replied.

'If they can do with you, they can do without you,' said the mother scornfully.

'That may be,' said the Cam, 'but I'll go and see.'

She carelessly pointed the way and he set off, arriving just in time to see the brothers in full flight; but hiding himself in a hollow, he sent his arrows with deadly effect among Clan Diarmid's foes. As their courage waned, so that of the

1/2000, Glen Taitneach.

brothers returned. The fight was resumed and victory won. When, on returning home, the Cam Ruadh's part in the fight was explained to the mother of the seven rescued men, she henceforth treated him with great kindness and respect but, with the perversity of her sex, she continued to excuse her conduct by saying that, although he was undoubtedly a hero, he did not have the outward appearance of one.

And so the reputation of the Cam Ruadh grew year by year, until one day he received a message from the Baron Reid of Balvarron, begging for his help. Strathardle, the most fertile of the glens within reach of Lochaber, had of late been subjected to raids of increasing daring and success. These had been carried out, as usual, by bands of marauding Campbells, and Baron Reid could think of no-one to stop them – except perhaps the cunning old fox from Glentaitneach.

The Cam sent back word that he would undertake the task required of him, and indeed ensure its success, but only on one condition. The Baron was to enclose with his cattle the oldest white cow or ox that he could find, and, when this had been done, word was to be sent to the Cam. At last the news came and the Cam looked at the moon. It was full and the caterans would not come just yet. But as it waned and the nights grew darker he set out for Strathardle. The cattle were enclosed as he had ordered, and with them a pure white cow which moved with the slow measured gait which befitted her age.

Each night the Cam waited, wrapped in a dark plaid, in a corner of the fold, but there was no sound save the soft breathing of the cattle. Then, at last, he heard what he had been waiting for – whispered commands and swift, quiet footsteps. He could see nothing of the baron's small black cattle or the dark plaids of the raiders, but the outline of the old white cow was plainly visible, moving slowly out of the enclosure towards the pass leading to Lochaber. Silently he followed, keeping level with the old cow and slightly to one side until, after a few miles, just as he had forseen, she began to fall behind the rest of the herd. The chief of the band became impatient – they had to be well on their way to Lochaber by dawn.

'Go you back, Duncan, and drive on the old cow.'

Duncan went back as he was bidden and the Cam heard his voice quietly urging on the aged beast, and the 'thwack' of his stick on her rump. His scheme was working perfectly. He could see the outline of the old cow in the dim light

Short-eared Owl
Glen Taitneach

and knew exactly the position of the invisible Duncan. One arrow only was needed, and Duncan's raiding days were over.

'Go back, Donald, and drive on the white cow, and see what has happened to that lazy brother of yours.'

So Donald went back, and John and James, until suspicion in the minds of the Campbells grew to certainty. The cattle of Strathardle were being protected by something more than mortal men. They fled, leaving their spoils, and never again dared to return and pit their wits against such an uncanny adversary.

John Grant, the Cam Ruadh, the one-eyed, red-haired man, against all the odds, reached old age and died peacefully in his bed in Glentaitneach. It was said in the last century, 'His descendants are still with us', and no doubt they are today.

10 *The '45 and After*

Basket hilted Sword

If you were to ask a hundred people in the world who was the most romantic figure in British history I believe ninety of them would say with me, 'Charles Edward Stuart – Bonnie Prince Charlie'.

The story of his bid to recover the throne of his ancestors is too well known to be repeated here, but what of the man himself?

He was as handsome as a Prince can be and every Scotsman knows the famous portrait of him in full Highland dress, with pale, haughty face and powdered wig. But this was before Culloden, and few know of the other Prince, 'The Wanderer', 'The Prince in the Heather', as he was after that terrible day in April 1746 – a bare-foot fugitive with a price on his head, lean, hard and sunburnt, with a long red beard, a gun in his hand and a pistol and dirk at his belt.

Yet it was this second Prince who inspired such passionate love and loyalty wherever he went in those desperate months of hide-and-seek in the mountains and islands of the west.

This is not a book about the Prince and we have little in common. He was young, handsome and royal and I am none of these things, but I am, by a devious route, descended from the Stuart kings and am proud to share a birthday with him on 20th December; so let me just tell you a few stories about him that you may not have heard. Perhaps they will also help to explain some of the strange happenings in the Glen in the years after 1745.

The most remarkable thing about him in all his wanderings was his unfailing good spirits. On one of the most dangerous and storm-tossed boat journeys, when the rowers were frightened and exhausted, he sang at the top of his voice to keep their spirits up, and in the most desperate moments of the pursuit he never lost his sense of humour.

GOLDEN EAGLE, Cornisk, SKYE.

P. Snow

When staying in Corradale, MacDonald of Clanranald brought him a suit of tartan clothes which pleased him enormously. 'Now,' he said, 'I only want the itch to be a complete Highlander!'

Later, when told that the Duke of Cumberland had put a price of £30,000 on his head, he immediately replied that he was putting a price of £30 on the head of King George.

As he journeyed across Skye with Flora MacDonald it was thought necessary to disguise him as a woman servant – Betty Burke. He was dressed in suitable clothes, but under his petticoat Charles wanted to wear a pistol. Flora, however, objected, saying that if he were searched the discovery of the pistol would give him away. To which he answered,

'Indeed, Miss, if we shall happen with any that will go so narrowly to work in searching me as what you mean, they will certainly discover me at any rate.'

It is said that the demure Miss Flora blushed with embarrassment at this slightly indelicate joke, but that afterwards, in later years, it became one of her favourite stories.

The role of an Irish maidservant was not one which suited the Prince, and more than once he had narrow escapes which, though nearly fatal at the time,

94

must in retrospect have caused him many a chuckle.

He walked with long manly strides, and once, when crossing a little stream on a Sunday evening, he greatly shocked the passers-by returning from Church by holding his skirts indecently aloft. He was sternly reprimanded by old MacDonald of Kingsburgh for this unladylike behaviour, and with such good effect that at the next stream he let his petticoat trail in the water. One cannot help feeling that this was just to tease his faithful old friend.

On a later occasion, when similarly disguised, he escaped detection by literally a matter of inches. He was then travelling as the servant of Captain Malcolm MacLeod of Raasay. They were staying at the house of Captain Malcolm's sister, and the Prince had fallen into a bog and become mired up to his thighs. Captain Malcolm, in pulling him out, had suffered a similar fate, but fortunately there was in the house a servant girl who spoke only the Gaelic, and she was ordered to fetch a tub of water to wash Malcolm's feet and legs. While she was engaged in this, Malcolm asked her to wash his servant's legs also. At first she indignantly refused this menial task, but in the end consented to do so. However, as this second cleaning operation proceeded, rather too thoroughly, the Prince became increasingly nervous and eventually, as he had no Gaelic, he was obliged to call out in an urgent voice, 'Oh, Mr MacLeod, will you please desire the girl not to go so far up!'

It was ten o'clock one evening when Charles, accompanied by MacDonald, Flora and one or two servants, arrived at Kingsburgh House. Mrs MacDonald was about to go to bed when her daughter rushed in saying, 'Oh, Mother, my father has brought in a very odd, muckle, ill-shaken-up wife as ever I saw! I never saw the like of her, and he has gone into the hall with her.'

Mrs MacDonald was greatly alarmed at this and her nervousness increased when she went to the hall door and looked in.

'For,' said she, 'I saw such an odd muckle trallop of a carlin, making lang, wide steps through the hall that I could not like her appearance at all.'

Eventually, she summoned up enough courage to enter the hall, whereupon the 'odd muckle trallop' rose to his feet and greeted her with a kiss. She trembled with fear on feeling a long stiff beard, but soon all was made clear to her and she hurried to prepare a simple supper.

When they had done, the Prince called for a dram, saying he would fill his own glass, 'For in my skulking I have learnt to take a hearty dram.'

As the evening wore on, they all became very merry and familiar and Mrs MacDonald pushed up the sleeve of the Prince's gown.

'And there I saw a bonny, clean white skin indeed. The deel a lady in a' the land has a whiter and purer skin than he has.'

At last they retired to rest and Charles slept between sheets for the first time since Culloden.

Next morning, Mrs MacDonald told Flora that she wished to have a lock of the Prince's hair and required her to go into his room and ask for it. This Flora refused to do, as he was not yet out of bed, but Mrs MacDonald took hold of her with one hand and knocked on the door with the other. The Prince called, 'Who is there?'

Mrs MacDonald, opening the door, said, 'Sir, it is I and I am importuning Miss Flora to come in and get a lock of your hair, and she refuses to do it.'

'Pray,' said Charles, 'desire Miss Flora to come in. What should make her afraid to come where I am?'

When she went in, he begged her to sit on a chair by the bedside and, laying his arms about her waist and his head in her lap, he desired her to cut the lock from his head with her own hands.

Half of this she gave to Mrs MacDonald and half she kept herself, and I have no doubt that these locks remained for ever the most treasured possessions of the two brave and adoring ladies.

The Prince was naturally reluctant to leave the comfort of Kingsburgh House, but was persuaded that this was necessary and, amid jokes and laughter, he was again dressed in the clothes of Betty Burke and set out for Portree.

When the Royal guest had left the house, Mrs MacDonald took the sheets from the bed where he had slept, folded them carefully and gave intructions to her daughter that they were to be kept, unwashed, and when she died her body was to be wrapped in them as a winding sheet. In due course her wishes were faithfully carried out.

After many more adventures and hardships, the final escape from Skye was arranged by the Laird of Mackinnon. This formidable chieftain was no longer young, but possessed a courage and strength which defied the years.

He provided a boat and four rowers and, with the Prince and Captain John Mackinnon, landed at Mallaig in the early hours of 5th July. The country around was bleak and almost deserted and was, moreover, unfamiliar to the Mackinnons. The nearest laird, MacDonald of Morar, was unwilling to help them and for the first time the Prince began to feel lonely and abandoned.

'I hope, Mackinnon, that you will not desert me,' he said, and the old man promised him with tears streaming down his face, 'I will never leave Your Royal Highness in the day of danger, but will, under God, do all I can for you and go with you wherever you order me.'

This moving expression of loyalty gave him fresh heart and he always retained special feelings of affection for this fine old man; but, fortunately, the next day the Prince was offered hospitality and shelter by Aeneas MacDonald of Borrodale, and it was now time for Mackinnon to return home.

It had always been the Prince's custom to bestow some small gift on those who had helped him – a brooch, a shoe buckle, or perhaps a few guineas, but now his purse was empty and as he bade an emotional farewell to the old chieftain he said, 'Mackinnon, I have nothing left to give you for all you have done for me, but here is the recipe for my own liqueur.'

It was, of course, Drambuie, and the secret still remains, as far as I know, with the Mackinnon family.

They parted, and Mackinnon set out for Skye. He never reached home, for next day he was taken prisoner and sent to one of the abominable prison hulks moored at Tilbury. Conditions on these filthy old ships were appalling and disease was rife, but he survived when others half his age were dying, and as he approached his seventieth year the authorities, no doubt thinking him by now a harmless old man, ordered his release.

The story has a happy ending, for he made his way back at once to his beloved island where he resumed his kilt, married a young wife and fathered a large and vigorous family. It was said that he lived in high spirits and with the most agreeable eccentricity.*

One cannot help wondering what part the Drambuie and the kilt played in this joyous and productive evening of his life, but one thing seems certain – never underestimate a Mackinnon from Skye.

As the relentless hunt went on and the Hanoverian soldiers scoured the hills and islands for the Prince, the Duke of Cumberland remained at Fort Augustus, waiting with growing impatience for news of his capture or death. He had offered a reward of £30,000 for the Prince, alive or dead, and as each detachment was sent out he gave the same command, 'Make no prisoners; you understand me'. They all had particular instructions to stab him should he fall into their hands. In his Germanic arrogance the duke felt certain that the truly vast reward would tempt someone, somewhere, to betray him, but the days lengthened to weeks and the weeks to months and no word came.

---

* *I can well believe this. The most eccentric man I ever knew was a descendant of his, Donald Mackinnon (from Skye of course). Son of one of my mother's best friends, he was a brilliant Don at Keble when I was a young man at Oxford after the war – a huge shambling bear who terrified female undergraduates by conducting his tutorials sitting under the table in his study, where the trembling young ladies were expected to join him. He once rose from this unusual position and exclaiming, 'My God, it's hot in here!' he shovelled all the burning coals from his fireplace out of the window into the quad. Luckily, the Dean was not passing underneath.*

Then there occurred probably the most dramatic act of self-sacrifice in the whole of the Prince's struggle for survival. He was in a cabin with one or two others including Roderick Mackenzie, a young man of good family who had served throughout the whole campaign in the Royal Lifeguards. He was of the Prince's size and closely resembled him in appearance.

Suddenly, they received warning that they were surrounded by a large detachment of English troops, advancing from all directions as if they had information that the Prince was in the cabin. Charles was asleep at the time and when awakened with the news that they were surrounded and escape was virtually impossible he answered, 'Then we must die like brave men, with swords in our hands!'

'No, my Prince,' replied Mackenzie, 'resources still remain. I will take your place and face one of these detachments. I know what my fate will be, but while I keep it employed Your Royal Highness will have time to escape.'

He darted from the cabin, sword in hand, and made a furious attack on the astonished English soldiers. He fought with the fury of a man with only moments to live, but it was one against fifty, and on falling, covered with wounds, he cried out, 'You know not what you have done! I am your Prince whom you have killed!'

Hardly believing their luck, the soldiers gathered round the dead man, staring down with a mixture of excitement, awe and a touch of sadness at his handsome young face. But they had their orders, and his head was cut off to be delivered to the Butcher in Fort Augustus.

Meanwhile, the Prince and the rest of the little party had slipped, unnoticed, out of the back of the cabin and disappeared in the hills.

When he received the head, Cumberland placed it in a box and, thinking that his work was done, set out for London. The hunt died down and the Prince was able to make his escape from Loch nan-Uamh in a French frigate.

It seems, however, that on his journey south, Cumberland decided to make absolutely certain that this was, indeed, the head of the Prince. Richard Morrison, the Prince's valet de chambre and barber, was at that time in prison in Carlisle, condemned to death, and when the duke reached Edinburgh he immediately sent a messenger with orders to postpone the execution and bring Morrison to London, to declare upon oath if this really were the head of the Prince: he was promised a pardon if he would speak the truth.

It was thought that Morrison would reach London about the same time as Cumberland, but he was taken ill with a fever on the way, and by the time he arrived the head was almost beyond recognition.

In the *Caledonian Mercury* of 15th May 1815 there was an article in which, after describing the delivery of the head to the Duke of Cumberland, it was said:

> At Edinburgh, it was thought proper to ascertain that it was really the Prince's head, and Richard Morrison, his barber, was sent to identify it. Fainting with horror, the poor man was shown the shocking spectacle. After examining it, he became satisfied, from some mole or other mark, that it was not the head of his master, but he had the presence of mind to conceal his feelings and only said that, although he was not able to swear to the identity of the head in that situation, the resemblance was so strong that no person would doubt that it was the head of Prince Charles. The evidence satisfied the butchers for the time and the fury of the pursuit abating, the Prince escaped to France. What his feelings were on returning to his hiding place in the hut and finding the mangled body of his friend, generous hearts may imagine, but few would be able to describe.

This story was well known in Scotland in the eighteenth and nineteenth centuries, and Richard Morrison's brother Robert lived for many years in the same house or, as they say in Edinburgh, 'on the same stair' as Roderick Mackenzie's two sisters. The Misses Mackenzie, he said, bore an excellent character and lived on a small annuity; but he never heard of what family they were, though it was respectable.*

The defeat of the Highland army at Culloden was followed by years of fierce repression and, by the Disarming Act of 1747, the clans were deprived of their weapons and also of the right of hunting and fishing; but what caused the greatest resentment of all, they were forbidden to wear their distinctive Highland dress. This rule applied throughout the mainland of Scotland but, whether by accident or design, the kilt was not proscribed in the Western Isles, and there is today lasting proof of the Highlander's love of his traditional dress.

---

* There is a memorial to Roderick Mackenzie in Glenmoriston. It bears the following inscription:

Here, in consecrated ground, rest the mortal remains of Roderick Mackenzie, merchant of Fisherrow and son of an Edinburgh jeweller, slain by Cumberland's Redcoat troops late in July, 1746, three months after the Battle of Culloden, because he selflessly encouraged them to mistake him for Prince Charles Edward Stuart whom he closely resembled in age, stature and colouring, and whom he served faithfully to the end. Tradition has it that his last words were *"You have killed your Prince"*: thus, by temporarily halting the manhunt, allowing the fugitive Prince precious days to make good his escape. Roderick Mackenzie's head was carried to Fort Augustus (some say thence to London) for identification. Local clansfolk are credited with removing his body a short distance from where he fell (now marked by the cairn across the road) and secretly burying it without a headstone, here, by Caochan a'Cheannaich (*Stream of the Merchant*). Every year, in July, there is a small gathering here attended by members of the 1745 Association and the *Clan Mackenzie Society* in order to honour the '*saddest and noblest of the Mackenzies*'.

THIS PLAQUE WAS KINDLY DONATED BY MRS NELLIE LEITCH, A DESCENDANT OF RODERICK MACKENZIE.

The island of Seil, just south of Oban, is separated from the mainland by a narrow stretch of water, spanned by one of General Wade's typically graceful stone bridges. On the island side of this bridge is an inn known as *Tigh-an-Truish*, or 'House of the Trousers', where islanders going to the mainland were obliged to exchange their kilts for the despised English garment. What joy and relief they must have felt on returning home, and what freedom for their hardy limbs!

Fortunately, no such restrictions exist today; and while on the subject of kilts, here is the good news. I once read, and have since had it confirmed by expert medical opinion, that the fertility of men is closely associated with the temperature of certain parts of the body, and can be greatly enhanced by a cool breeze caressing their nether regions, and for this reason, if for no other, I recommend the wearing of this romantic and colourful garment.

After the passing of the Act, many thousands of families emigrated to the New World, but those who were left behind were insensed by the penalties they had to endure, and it was only natural that from time to time there were acts of revenge.

One of the Braemar Mackenzies who fought so bravely on Drumossie Moor and came home again was known as Donald Dubh an t-Ephiteach (Black Donald the Egyptian) on account of his dark and swarthy appearance. He was an ardent Jacobite and, as such, was singled out for persecution by the garrison of Braemar Castle. One sergeant in particular made a point of breaking into the house of his aged mother and boasting what he would do to the Ephiteach if he could only meet him alone. The old lady, on instructions from her son, at last informed the sergeant that this could be arranged if he would go to a certain spot in Coire-nam-muc, provided he went alone and without firearms. The sergeant immediately threw down his gun and set off, and the Ephiteach, who was perched on the top of the box bed and had heard the whole conversation, swiftly followed. They met in the corrie and, without a word, drew their swords, and the long-awaited duel began.

You will not be surprised to hear that Donald quickly disarmed his opponent and then sent him crashing to the ground with a blow from the pommel of his sword. Before he could recover, his hands were firmly tied behind his back.

'Now, Sergeant,' said the Ephiteach, 'suppose you had me as I have you, what would you do?'

'Indeed,' replied his victim, 'I would kill you.'

'Well, as you have been so candid I will spare your life, but you will remember the Ephiteach till the last day of it.'

So saying, he removed all the sergeant's clothes, leaving not a stitch on his back, rolled them into a bundle and hung them round his neck. He then cut some supple birch twigs, and with the help of these encouraged the naked and unhappy soldier all the way back to the gates of the Castle.

The efforts of the garrison to capture Donald Dubh an t-Ephiteach were redoubled, and it is not surprising that his hatred of the Redcoats increased in proportion.

Soon after these events, the wife of one of the English officers, who was expecting a child, had to be sent south so that when the time came she could have expert medical attention, a luxury not readily available in Braemar in those days. Her husband, Captain Miller, 'Muckle Miller' as he was called, decided that he would ride south with her through Glenshee.

The Ephiteach, who had got wind of the intended journey, lay in wait on the Cairnwell. When the Captain appeared on a garron with his wife mounted behind him, he sprang up with a levelled gun.

'Swords and fair play!' cried Miller, who was a fine handsome man and an expert with that weapon, perhaps even a match for his famous adversary.

'Such play,' replied the Ephiteach, 'as you give my countymen – shoot them down! bayonet them!'

He fired, and Captain Miller's grave could be seen until quite recently in the heather beside the road on the Cairnwell.

Donald Dubh then mounted the garron and escorted the lady to the Rhidorrach. As they trotted down the long winding road together, they became quite friendly, so friendly in fact that before they arrived she even suggested that, now she was a widow, she should become the wife of the Ephiteach himself. In view of what had just happened, he expressed some surprise at the idea but she gaily replied, 'Oh, there is nothing very strange about it at all. Captain Miller killed my first husband!'

Donald Dubh firmly declined to become number three. He left the gallant widow at the Rhidorrach and disappeared into the hills.

The inevitable day came, however, when the Ephiteach did not escape. He and his cousin, Mac Robaidh Mhoir, were brought in chains to Invercauld, but it seems that some formalities had to be performed before they could be executed and, as the commander of the garrison was away in Aberdeen, they were thrown into a dungeon to await his return.

Now Invercauld did not at all approve of this sort of treatment for his countrymen, and when he heard that the two famous cousins were in his dungeon, he sent them word that there would be feasting and revelry that evening, and all through the night, to celebrate the accession of the king.

Like all lairds at that time he had his own 'still', and as the singing and feasting and dancing went on he made sure there was no interruption to the flow of *uisge beatha*, or 'water of life' as indeed it was to prove for the two Highlanders. Cogie after cogie of his best whisky went round and round and round again, till the whole world was spinnmg. By morning, the guards were unconscious – totally, utterly, paralytically drunk. With a kick the Ephiteach split the dungeon door, and with another Mac Robaidh made the splinters fly. Manacled as they were, it was away, away to the hills where friends were waiting. There too was the blacksmith of Auchindrine with hammer and file, and in moments their freedom was complete.

A second and more mysterious murder was that of Sergeant Davies, who commanded a military post at the Clachan of Inverey on Upper Deeside. It was the practice of the small Highland garrisons to meet with one another at some convenient spot halfway between their stations, and the garrisons at Inverey and the Spital met twice a week at the head of Glenclunie.

On 28th September 1749, they made their rendezvous as usual, but Sergeant Davies, being a sportsman, decided not to return at once to Inverey, but to go deerstalking instead. He set off alone and was never seen again.

Nine months later, the son of Farquharson in whose house Davies had lodged, received a message from a shepherd in Glenclunie that he had something to say to him. This was that when he had gone to his shieling on the Hill of Christie, he had been visited by the sergeant's ghost who entreated him to bury his bones, and told him where to find them. Young Farquharson and the shepherd did as the ghost had bidden and buried the bones in a grave in the peat moss. The ghost had also told the shepherd that the murder had been committed by two men who were hunting on the hill on that day, Clark and MacDonald.

Five years later, these two men were apprehended and tried in the High Court of Justice. They were defended by Mr Robert MacIntosh, son of the laird of Dalmunzie, and the trial created widespread interest. After a deal of confusing and unlikely evidence the verdict of the jury was 'not guilty'. The shepherd had sworn in evidence that the ghost spoke 'as good Gaelic as ever he heard in Lochaber'.

'Pretty well,' remarked MacIntosh to his friend Sir Walter Scott after the trial, 'Pretty well for the ghost of an English sergeant!'

Revenge, however, did not always extend to such lengths as murder, and on a lighter note is the story of one of the Ramsays who farmed Liannoch Mor near the Spital. As I have said, there was a garrison at the Spital and one day they commandeered some hay belonging to Ramsay and ordered him to carry it over the river on a plank of wood which was the only footbridge in those parts. Ramsay crossed the plank, closely followed by two or three soldiers, but once on the other side he dropped his burden, siezed the end of the plank and tumbled the soldiers, muskets and all, into the water. He knew, of course, how long it would take them to renew their priming, and by the time they had done so he had escaped up the shoulder of Bengulbein. We do not know what punishment, if any, he received, but at least he left the garrison in no doubt where his sympathies lay.

It was about this time that the military road to Braemar was being laid and there were a great many engineers engaged on the work. One of these officers and his wife were lodged at Laganagraine, and there a child was born to them. Naturally they wished to have it baptised, but for some reason the minister was not available. Alexander Ramsay, however, in whose house they lived, volunteered to perform the task and 'In the Name of the King and by his authority' he christened the child. The officer thanked him, saying, 'It is well and quickly done,' but added, 'I fear it will have to be done again.'

11 *An Ancient Sword*

The Highlanders of bygone days were all *ceithern*, and their weapons were as much a part of them as their clothes. No-one will ever know how many swords and dirks were hidden in thatch and turf rick after the Disarming Act of 1747, but one superb antique sword came to light in Glen Taitneach in the early years of the twentieth century.

Its discovery and a detailed description of it were recorded in 1929 by the Reverend T.D. Miller, former Minister in Glenshee. He writes:

> While no-one would be surprised were old swords or dirks discovered on the track frequented by the caterans, there was found in June 1905, in a peat moss in a small hollow near the foot of Glen Taitneach, two and a quarter miles north west from the Spital, an old claymore which has aroused much curiosity.
>
> The sword was found by Thomas Ramsay, a native of Glenshee, a son of Miller Ramsay, when cutting peats for Charles Robertson, gamekeeper on the property, whose son Alexander, then a lad, was also present. The following is Ramsay's description of the finding: 'My spade first laid bare the tang and cross-guard; seeing that it was a sword I proceeded with great care. It was covered with peat, above which was a long cairn of stones of from seven to about thirty pounds, which were partly sunk into and were mostly grown over by the peat. The depth of the sword was in all about two feet three inches. It lay with the point towards the west, and was embedded in a thick layer of tallow or other grease. The sword was sheathed. The sheath was of oak, most of which crumbled away on

(Above) Claymore found in Glenshee in 1905. (Royal Museum of Scotland)

exposure to the air. The photograph shows the small fragments of the sheath I was able to save. The grip round the tang had entirely rotted away. The pommel was not found. Notwithstanding the protecting mass of grease, the sword was terribly rusted. I found it broken across, four and a quarter inches from the point, the parts being only slightly separated. Believing that the sword had been placed over the grave of a deceased warrior, and that the stones had been placed to mark the grave, or possibly to prevent the body being dug up and devoured by wolves, I dug under where the sword lay to a depth of upwards of two feet, but found no trace of human remains or anything else other than the hard subsoil'.

Major Chalmers, himself an expert swordsman, took an early opportunity of examining this interesting find and came to the conclusion that it was much the oldest sword he had ever seen. Viewing it in this light, he persuaded Charles Robertson to hand it over to Major Pullar, Dunbarney, whom he knew to be a collector of ancient weapons. Knowing its value and the interest it would arouse among fellow collectors and others, Major Pullar sent it on exhibition to the then National Museum of Antiquities, George Street, Edinburgh, its proper repository. In the report of the Transactions of the Society it is stated:

> This fine sword has a total length of three feet six and a half inches, the length of the handle, measured on the tang, (which is all that remains), is eight and three-quarter inches, and the breadth of the blade at insertion in the guard is one and three-quarter inches, tapering regularly to a thin and slightly rounded point three-eighth inch in breadth. A few inches of the point end are unfortunately separated from the blade; and the few fragments that were saved of the wood which seems to have formed the mounting of the grip. At about a third of the length of the blade from the handle is a mark inlaid in yellow metal, but so much hidden as to be made out only by careful scrutiny.

Mr Guy F. Laking, M.V.O., F.S.A., Keeper of the King's Armoury and author of *The Armoury of Windsor Castle*, writing to Professor Fenton, from whom he had received a photograph of the sword, says:

> I am greatly interested in the photograph of the Highland *Claidheamh-mor*. Indeed, I consider it one of the most interesting Scottish weapons I have ever seen. The coarseness of its make, together with certain technical peculiarities, lead me to believe it to be one of the most primitive of its particular type of weapon. I think it would be quite safe to assign

it to a date probably within the first quarter of the fifteenth century, or possibly of the last years of the preceding century.

It will be noted that the customary pierced trefoil ends of the guillons seen on the Highland two-handed swords of the latter part of the fifteenth century have not yet, in this specimen, made their appearance. Also, by the photograph, it is interesting to note that the projecting lug from the centre of the guillon lying upon the face of the blade is roughly forged in a separate piece, and not, as in the later specimens, drawn out of the guillons themselves.

Of course, it is much to be regretted that the pommel is missing. Doubtless it was a small iron or even bronze pommel of wheel form, but very deep in section.

Of course, there exist a few (very few) single-handed Scottish weapons anterior to this date, but they are of a somewhat different type, and appear to be derived from the Scandinavian sword of the eleventh or twelfth century.

I believe the sword of which you have sent me a photograph is unique. It indeed forms a valuable link in the series of weapons we are acquainted with. I wish it were possible to see more clearly the inlaid design on the centre of the blade. The mark means nothing beyond being an early form of decoration for the blade.

The photograph referred to by Mr Laking is, of course, the black and white one reproduced here which was taken soon after the discovery of the sword. The more recent photograph of the tang and cross guard was given to me by Dr David Caldwell, Curator of the Scottish Medieval Collections at the National Museums of Scotland. Dr Caldwell writes:

It is a rare example of a Scottish medieval sword, dating to the fifteenth century. Although it is a single-handed weapon, the form of its guard relates it to the more well-known two-handed swords (claymores) used by Highlanders from the second half of the fifteenth century through to the early seventeenth century.

How this fascinating and unique weapon, one of the rarest of its kind in Scotland, came to be hidden in the peat moss, one can only conjecture. The fact that it was carefully packed in a thick layer of grease and its hiding place was marked by a cairn of stones shows that the owner certainly meant to recover it at a later date. We know that, after 1747, there was a Hanoverian garrison at the Spital, and that one of the main duties of these garrisons was to enforce the

Disarmament Act, so it seems likely that what must have been a treasured possession was hidden to prevent it from falling into the hands of the Government. Whether the owner forgot about it or, what is more likely, feared to be found with it in his possession, it lay in the peat moss for over a hundred and fifty years, but those of you who wish to see it can now do so in the Royal Museum of Scotland, Chambers Street, Edinburgh.

The Dalmunzie sword, however, is not the only rare find to have been discovered in Glenshee. About the middle of the nineteenth century, a ghillie by the name of Grewar, a noted stalker and probably the grandfather of 'Old Grewar', discovered in a cave on the side of Ben Gulbein a bundle of weapons, rusty and decayed, which were supposed to have belonged to the Cam Ruadh. If so, they would have been of incomparable interest to local historians and the inhabitants of the Glen, but unfortunately Grewar parted with them, for a consideration, to one of the shooting tenants, and now no-one knows what became of them.

Some years after this – it must have been about 1870 – another dirk and an old gun were found in a cave on Athole, and this remarkable story you will find in the chapter about John Farquharson.

The only other weapon of any interest to have been found in Glenshee was discovered by myself. Finegand is a very old house, and when I returned to live there I explored every corner of it. I knew that it had been used by Montrose as a hideaway during the Civil War, and it did not surprise me that there was a small underground room whose door did not appear to have been opened for many years. Of course, this very fact aroused my curiosity, and after some effort I managed to force it open. With the aid of a torch I explored the tiny room and to my delight found two objects – an old iron plate and, what to me was a real treasure, a beautiful old double-barrel, muzzle-loading shotgun. It must have lain there for over a hundred years, but was still in good condition. I cleaned it with loving care and tried the ramrod in both barrels. One quite clearly still had the charge in it – and it still has. I could not extract it. I guess the date it was made was about 1820 and it is the most beautifully balanced gun I have ever handled. I wish I knew who the maker was. He was too modest to engrave his name, but he was a true master of his craft.

12 *God Save the Queen*
and other Victorian Tales

It was in 1842 that Queen Victoria made her first visit to Scotland. It was to prove the most important journey of her life. She was enchanted by both the country and the people and so, to her delight, was Prince Albert. Further visits followed and were faithfully recorded in her diaries.

I have heard it said that on all her many journeys through the country, whenever the coach stopped to change horses, she would write at top speed, capturing her impressions of the scenery and the people while these were still fresh in her mind, and this spontaneous enthusiasm shines through all her writing. Time and again we read of her growing love of the Highlands and her admiration and affection for their people:

Wednesday, September 11, 1844
The country from (Dundee) to Cupar Angus is very well cultivated, and you see the hills in the distance. The harvest is only now being got in, but is very good; and everything much greener than in England. Nothing could be quieter than our journey, and the scenery is so beautiful! It is very different from England: all the houses built of stone; the people so different, – sandy hair, high cheekbones; children with long shaggy hair and bare legs and feet; little boys in kilts. Near Dunkeld, and also as you get more into the Highlands, there are prettier faces. Those jackets which the girls wear are so pretty; all the men and women, as well as the children, look very healthy.

Thursday, October 3, 1844
The English coast appeared terribly flat. Lord Aberdeen was quite touched when I told him I was so attached to the dear, dear Highlands and missed

the fine hills so much. There is a great peculiarity about the Highlands and Highlanders; and they are such a chivalrous, fine, active people. Our stay among them was so delightful … Independently of the beautiful scenery, there was a quiet, a retirement, a wildness, a liberty, and a solitude that had such a charm for us.

Soon the royal couple began to plan a home of their own in the Highlands. However, young as they were, both suffered from twinges of rheumatism and the Royal doctor, Sir James Clark, had to be consulted as to the area with the most suitable climate. His emphatic choice was Deeside, and in 1848, at the suggestion of Lord Aberdeen, a lease was purchased of the Balmoral estate. In September the Royal Family arrived. It was love at first sight and the Queen wrote, 'All seemed to breathe freedom and peace and to make one forget the world and its sad turmoils.'

But, delightful as the old castle was, it proved too small for the royal household, and purchase of the freehold became a priority so that a new house could be built. Prince Albert was always in a hurry as if he could foresee his early death, but he had to wait for nearly four years before a price could be agreed with the trustees of the Duke of Fife. Then, on 22nd June 1852, the Balmoral estate passed into Royal hands. Immediately, Sir Gilbert Scott was commissioned as the architect of the present magnificent building. It was completed in 1857, and for the rest of her life the Queen was never happier than when living there.

During these early years, and especially before the railway reached Ballater, the journeys to and from Balmoral were made through Glenshee, and the Queen herself describes the first of these. The Royal Family had stayed the previous night at the George Inn in Perth and she writes in her diary:

Wednesday, August 15, 1849.
At a quarter to eight, we started. The two boys and Vicky were in the carriage with us. Alice followed with the ladies. It was a long journey, but through very beautiful scenery. We saw the Grampians as we left Perth. We first changed horses at Blairgowrie, 15 miles. Then came a very long stage of 20 miles to the Spital of Glenshee. We first passed the house of a Lieut.-Colonel Clark Rattray, called Craig Hall, overhanging a valley or glen above which we drove, and after this we came into completely wild Highland scenery, with barren rocky hills through which the road winds to the Spital of Glenshee, which scarcely can be called a village as it consists of only an inn and two or three cottages.

We got out at the inn where we found Mr Farquharson (of Invercauld) and his son and some of his men. Here we had some luncheon, and then set off again. The next stage of 15 miles to Castleton is over a very bad and at night positively dangerous road through wild grand scenery, with many abrupt turns and steep ascents. One steep turn is called The Devil's Elbow. The Farquharson men joined us again here, some having gone on before and others having followed from the inn, skipping over stones and rocks with the rapidity and lightness peculiar to Highlanders. They remained with us till we were able to trot on again. We drove through a very fine pass called the Cairn Wall.

From then on, it became the custom, when the Queen travelled up or down, for the laird of each district through which she passed, or, if he were not available, some gentleman appointed by him, to accompany the royal carriage on horseback. William Shaw, the tenant of Finegand, held this office for some years over the stretch of road from Persie to the Spital, a distance of about ten miles. The most dangerous part of this road is the Lair Brae at the foot of Glenshee. Here there was a very steep descent with, at the bottom, a sharp right turn and a narrow bridge. On one journey south, the horses of the Royal carriage took

The Braemar coach passing Finegand, 1907

fright and careered down the hill in spite of all the efforts of the postilions to stop them. Will Shaw spurred his horse to a gallop and, overtaking the near leader, seized hold of its bridle and brought the carriage to a halt. Knowing, probably better than the Royal party themselves, the danger they had been in, he used to declare with pride that he had once saved the Queen's life.

On another occasion, when the Royal carriage stopped at the Spital to take on fresh horses, one of the small company gathered there had the nerve to go forward and put his hand on the door to get a better look at the occupants. Will Shaw immediately rode forward and, raising his heavy riding whip, cried out:

'Stand back, you rascal, or I'll crack your crown!'
As he turned away, he heard the Queen say to Prince Albert,
'What did the gentleman say about the Crown?'

Many years later, I think it was in 1931, another royal party set out from Glamis on a journey to Balmoral. For some reason, either to save time or even perhaps to amuse the children, the decision had been made to take a short cut which meant crossing the river Shee by a ford on our land, just above Dalnaglar. Although it was summer, it had been raining hard (General Wade would not have been surprised. He once remarked that the climate in the Highlands consisted of nine months of winter and three of wet weather) and the river was in spate. The chauffeur misjudged the depth of the water and the big car, with its occupants, came to rest half way across, with the water swirling round its doors. Father, who was fishing a little way off, recognised the party and shouted that he would go for help. He ran back to the farm and fetched Johnny Lamond and a pair of horses. They hurried back and he and Johnny, neither of whom could swim, waded into the swollen river with the horses, somehow managed to attach chains to the car, and towed it to the bank.

Knowing the ford as I do, I believe the danger to the royal party was not too great as long as they remained in the car, but Father for years dined out on the story of how he had saved the Duke and Duchess of York and the two little princesses and

> Remembered with advantages
> What feats he did that day.

Returning to Queen Victoria's day, there was, a few miles south of the Lair Brae, the old House of Dalrulzion, occupied by Miss Rattray, an aged Highland lady. In order to see the Queen pass and pay her respects to the Roal party, she had given orders for her high-backed chair to be placed at her gateway, and when the carriage appeared she rose to make her curtsey. When the Queen saw the silver-haired old lady, she ordered the carriage to be stopped and told the young Prince of Wales and the Princess Royal to stand up so that the old lady might see them better. Miss Rattray then invoked the Blessing of God on the Queen, the Prince Consort 'and their beautiful children'.

The Queen exclaimed, 'Dear old lady! Dear old lady!' and resumed her journey.

One day, when taking a drive from Balmoral with some of her guests, the queen was tempted by the sunshine to venture further than was originally intended; so much further, in fact, that it was feared the horses would not be able to complete the return journey. An attendant was therefore sent to a farm to ask for fresh horses. The farmer explained that he had only one pair of carriage horses, but promised that if these were put on the wheel and Her Majesty's leaders retained, they would take the carriage safely home. The attendant demurred, saying that Her Majesty required two pairs. The farmer, however, said, 'I will speak to the Queen about it.'

He did so, and the Queen said it was an excellent arrangement. After the horses had been yoked and the royal party had driven off, he returned to the house saying to his wife, 'When I explained the thing to Her Majesty, she said she would do just what I told her. She seems to be a very sensible lady!'

At this time there was, in Glenshee, only one postal delivery in two days, and it was the Queen herself who, quite unconsciously, helped to improve this situation. One of her Ministers was always in attendance while she was at Balmoral, and it so happened that one of these, Lord John Manners, the Postmaster General, had a summer residence at Birnam. Making arrangements for his journey to Balmoral, he wrote one Friday to the proprietor of the lnvercauld Arms at the Spital of Glenshee, requesting him to have luncheon ready and a pair of fresh horses for the Braemar stage on the following Monday. His letter lay during Saturday and Sunday at Bridge of Cally, and on the Monday he passed the post-runner with it in his bag somewhere between Persie and Glenshee. On his arrival at the Spital, he found, to his surprise and annoyance, that there was no luncheon and no fresh horses waiting for him. The following day, a letter was dispatched to Lord John containing his own postmarked envelope and expressing regret for what had happened and pointing out the inconvenience of the existing arrangements. Within a week, a Postal Inspector arrived from Edinburgh, and a few weeks later an additional foot-post was appointed, and thereafter the post arrived every day.

The foot-post was for many years a steady, rather simple-minded man known to all as 'Peter'. In his collection of pennies for stamps he one day discovered a coin which had been skilfully altered to show the figure of Britannia on both sides. This was a great piece of luck, and he found it very useful in obtaining occasional refreshment on his rounds. One day, however, he gave the invaluable coin away by mistake in giving some change. The loss was more than he could bear, and he wrote to the Master of the Mint requesting him to coin two pennies, one with two heads and one with two tails, frankly confessing that they were to be used 'for tossing purposes'. To his amazement, a fortnight later he received a letter from the head office in Edinburgh dispensing with his services in a month's time. He was, however, an honest old man and liked and trusted by the people he served. A petition was signed by all and sent to the postal authorities, with the result that 'Peter' was re-instated, but ever after he tossed on equal terms with his associates.

One of the keepers in the Glen was named Sandie Duff, but on account of his surname he was known locally as 'Lord Fife'. One day, at an auction at the Spital, a cow came under the hammer. Someone called out, 'Wha got the coo?' The auctioneer replied, 'Lord Fife.' At this an elderly gentleman sprang from a seat in front of the hotel and declared in forceful language that he had nothing to do with the cow, did not want it and refused to receive it. It was, of course, the Earl of Fife who was travelling north, and he laughed heartily when he was told that the purchaser of the cow was his neighbour's keeper, Sandie Duff.

The education of the children of the Glen was at this time in the hands of a conscientious old pedagogue named Alexander Wilson who, for most of his life, received the inadequate salary of £30 a year, on which he brought up a family of two sons and two daughters. However, he lived comfortably enough due to the kindness of his neighbours who made generous contributions to his larder. Whenever a sheep or bullock was killed, a portion of it was set aside for the schoolmaster and this, with gifts of meal and potatoes, made sure that he and his family were always well fed. In addition, when the children came to school in the morning, each of them carried two peats, one for the schoolroom fire and one for the teacher's household hearth.

I have read a number of old Charlie Lamond's letters, and the clarity and style of these are a tribute to the skill with which Alexander Wilson imparted at least one of the three Rs to his pupils. With the passing of the Scottish Education Act in 1872, his salary was increased to £100 a year, but the good old man had by then become so used to a life of thrift and care that he declared he did not know what to do with so much money. He had no Gaelic and, although most of his pupils spoke it at home, they were not encouraged to do so at school and this no doubt contributed to the fact that by the early years of this century it had all but disappeared from the Glen.

The last member of my family to speak and write fluently in the old tongue was the Reverend Alexander Mackenzie. His first wife died leaving him with three small children, and when he married for the second time he wrote rather pathetically in the family bible, 'Jany 9th 1801. A. Mackenzie and Miss Sarah Wilson were married *(Air mo sgath fein agus air sgath mo chloinne).** The only child of this second marriage was Mary Anne Mackenzie, once described as 'A bonny woman of ample proportions, mother of thirteen children who all grew up with constitutions of iron'. If Alexander had lived to see his grandchildren, I'm sure he would have been proud of them, and if he had been present at the last family ceilidh at Finegand, he would have met over a hundred of his descendants.

---

* *For my sake and for the sake of my children.*

13 *Stones and Stone Circles*

In the parish of Kirkmichael there is a remarkable group of stone circles and cairns situated on the moor just to the north of Persie and about a mile west of the main road as it passes Bleaton Hallet.

Unfortunately for the historian, much of the area is now covered by coniferous woods, but luckily we have a detailed description of it from the Reverend T. D. Miller who wrote in 1929:

> The chief feature of the group is a huge cairn or circular table of stones, 270 feet in circumference and 25 feet in height. Round this great heap stand a large number of smaller cairns. About two hundred yards further west are the remains of two concentric circles, the larger one being about 50 feet in diameter and the inner one 32 feet. In the vicinity there are other smaller circles. About a mile to the north stands a great rolling stone, estimated to weigh three tons, which can be oscillated with some little pressure, and a hundred yards north west of it are several pairs of concentric circles similar in dimension to the others.

Similar cairns to these mark the sites of major battles fought centuries ago, and although there is no indication on any of these stones as to what they commemorate, it has long been my belief that they mark the site of the Battle of Mons Graupius, and that 'Mons Graupius' is, in fact, Mount Blair.

Students of Roman history will remember that although Tacitus, in his 'Agricola', described the battle and its gory aftermath in great detail (*caesa hostium ad decem milium … passim arma et corpora et laceri artus et cruenta humus* – the enemy's slain amounted to ten thousand men … everywhere were weapons, corpses, severed limbs and blood on the ground), he is always tantalizingly vague in his geography, and the exact location of his father-in-law's famous victory has never been finally identified.

Many sites, including Durno in Aberdeenshire, have been suggested, but the plain below Mount Blair fits Tacitus' description as well as any. Mount Blair marks the southern edge of the Grampian Mountains, and one clue which supports my theory is that, in the first printed edition of the works of Tacitus, the *'editio princeps'* of Puteolanus, the script reads, '(Agricola) ... *ad montem Grampium pervenit'*.

Another interesting site further north in the middle of Glenshee is Broughdearg. The word *brough* means a circular encampment, while *dearg* signifies red, and is sometimes used to mean bloodstained which, in this context, may well be the true meaning. On the south side of the steading are the remains of two stone circles or *cromlechs*. Unfortunately, of the larger one, which must have measured some sixty feet in diameter, only two stones remain upright. Both are six feet in height with girths of nine feet and eight feet. All the other stones of this circle have been used for building purposes. One can be seen in the foundation of the stackyard wall, and the others have been used to build the limekiln which is thirty feet in diameter.

The other circle, lying a few yards to the north-east in a small fir wood, has half a dozen of the outer stones remaining, along with the central flat stone, but these have all been thrown down and are sinking into the ground.

The westernmost stone of the larger cromlech has a groove round it as if to hold an iron band or chain, and the foot of the stone is blackened and firecracked – a combination which led the Reverend T. D. Miller to suggest that it had been a place of execution or sacrifice. When I lived at Finegand my neighbours at Broughdearg were Sandy and Diana Grant and their children, but they never spoke about the stone circles, and after my experiences at Corrydon I was unwilling to raise the subject with them. What I can say is that they were a happy and contented family who enjoyed living there, and were some of the best friends I have ever had.

As well as the stone circles, there are in the Glen a number of other large stones which have stories attached to them. The most famous of these is, of course, the Clach-na-Coileach which I have already told you about, but opposite to it on the other side of the river is a huge rock known as Clach Void or the Stone of Justice, which marks the spot where the chief of the clan heard disputes and dispensed justice in an autocratic but effective way. His word was law and from his decision there was no appeal.

To the east of Inveredrie Farm, and at the north end of Loch Shechernich or Bainne, there is another remarkable stone in which there is a long winding hole which once served as a place of refuge for one of the local witches. It seems that she had been blamed by the local laird for causing the death of his infant son, and one day he found her alone on the hill. He immediately drew his sword to slay her, but he was not quite quick enough. Seeing her danger, she instantly changed herself into a viper and slid into the hole in the rock. The laird, in his fury and frustration, hacked at the rock with his claymore and the marks of his attack can still be seen. From her place of concealment, the witch tried to reason with him and hinted at the folly of brooding over an old injury.

'Laird,' she called out, 'As long as you look at your cradle and I at my stone, we may meet and crack, but we can never be friends.'

The boulder is known as Clach-na-Nathraiche or the Serpent's Stone, and it bears witness to the weight of the laird's claymore and the soundness of the witch's philosophy.

In Glen Taitneach there is yet another stone with a story. The service of the parish midwife had been required in one of the shielings, and a neighbour had brought her from her cottage some miles off on his pony. When she alighted on the stone, she asked him what she could do to thank him and he replied, 'if she would warn him of any death in his family'. She told him he would be warned by the squealing of a pig, and at that moment a little pig ran in under the stone, which got the name of Clach-na-Meicke-breac or the Stone of the Little Spotted Pig. Some time during the last century, the farmer at the Old Spital removed the stone for the foundation of a dyke, but shortly after he did so a murrain broke out among his cattle and he thought it wise to replace it.

On the west side of the Parish Church, and on the top of a little gravel hill, there is an upright pillar of soft slate which stands about six feet in height and is a little over two feet in breadth. It is sup-posed to mark an ancient meeting place, and is, indeed, ideally situated for such a purpose, being at the junction of the two upper Glens. It is a prominent feature in the watercolour painting of the Wade bridge, and it is quite possible that religious services may have been held around it before the building of the first chapel.

Finally, on the subject of standing stones, I must tell you one of my father's stories which has always amused me since I was seven or eight years old. You will have gathered from all I have told you that the raiders and thieves who preyed on the Mackenzies and Ogilvies in Glenshee and Glenisla were all

Campbells, and we did not have much love for this clan. Father told us children that there were more standing stones in Argyle and Lochaber than in any other part of Scotland, and that these had been erected by a benevolent duke for the benefit of his unwashed clansmen, and that these verminous gentlemen, as they travelled across the treeless moors, would rub their itching backs on the stones, murmuring gratefully as they did so, *'Beannachd Dhe air Mac Cailein!'* ('God Bless the Duke of Argyle!').

Glenshee Church,
Spittal of Glenшee
Perth.

14 John Farquharson

Peregrine Falcon . &.

There are those who have broken the law by stealing from the rich, but who have also stolen the hearts and imagination of people down the ages by the courage, generosity and romance of their lives.

To the names of Robin Hood and Dick Turpin I would add those of John Farquharson and Alexander Davidson. They were poachers it is true, but poachers so strangely and picturesquely different from the ordinary variety as to be almost a poetic ideal of such men. No doubt they knew the old Gaelic saying 'A stag from the hill, a hazel stick from the wood and a fish from the river are the right of every man'. They genuinely believed that all creatures living in the wild were for the benefit of all mankind and both were filled, not with a love of money, but with Man's love of the chase, its thrills, its challenges and its ultimate climax. They stalked and shot with cheerful abandon from the hills of Athole to the Braes of Mar, and not a ghillie or keeper in all that wild country could come near them.

Alexander Davidson was a Braemar man and there is no space here to deal with his exploits, but I have been told that John Farquharson lived for some years at Tynellan, and as many of his adventures were in Glenshee, I will give you some account of them as recorded by his friend and contemporary, William M'Combie Smith.

He was born in or about 1825 at Daldhu in Glenfernate and was, I suppose, an infinitely distant relative of mine because we are both descended from Finla Mor. Farquharson was immensely proud of this, and as a boy was taught to repeat the names of all the MacFinlas and MacIans through whom he traced his descent from that great Chieftain.

To understand his attitude to the chase, you must know that the farm where he was raised was on the very boundary of Athole deer forest, and that it has been stated on good authority that, 'There was no let of shootings before 1805, when one near the Bridge of Tummel was let to Sir Fletcher Norton for £5'. Even as late as 1833 'A stranger could fish and shoot over almost any part of the Highlands without interruption', and this was the natural belief of John Farquharson.

He began shooting with a bow and arrow and was still a child when he fired his first shot with a gun. He had been out with a party on a fox hunt, and on the way home he spotted a mountain hare lying in its form. He had left his bow and arrow at home, but one of the party offered to lend him a double-barrel gun with both at full cock. He took careful aim and pulled both triggers. He was knocked head over heels backwards and rose with a bloody nose, but what of that? He had shot a hare and carried it home in triumph. Soon he could bring down a grouse on the wing, and then he had only to kill a stag to become a fully-fledged free forester.

However, as the value of grouse moors and deer forests increased, so did the care with which they were preserved, and Farquharson decided that the best way he could satisfy his sporting instincts was to become a gamekeeper. He had no trouble in finding a place with Lord Abercromby, and later with Lord Rosebery. It was during this time that he first began to acquire fame as a rifle shot, astonishing his competitors by lying flat on his back, resting the rifle across his body and passing his left arm over to his right shoulder and so securing a steady aim which sent every shot to the centre of the target. It is said that Farquharson discovered this position accidentally when deerstalking. When lying on his back with his rifle beside him, a stag came within range and as he could not change his position without being seen, he had to fire as he lay or lose the stag. He found he had never held the rifle steadier or seen the sights better, and when I shot at Bisley in the 1940s and 1950s this was the only position used when shooting at 1000 and 1100 yards.

'Blue' Hare, April.

Farquharson's career as a competition shot reached its climax in 1869 when he went to Belgium and won the King of the Belgians' Championship Gold

Medal, beating all the best shots in Europe, so that he had a good claim to be the best rifle shot in the Old World, if not in the whole world, that year.

When he left Lord Rosebery's service he became head keeper to a Mr Dalgleish in Argyle, but as that gentleman gave no holidays to attend rifle meetings, Farquharson left his employment and started on his life as a 'free shot' among his beloved mountains. It is these adventures which make up the happiest and most unforgettable period of his life.

LONAVEY, A POACHER OF THE OLDEN TIME

In the seventeenth century there were two noted poachers who exercised the right of free forestry in Athole and Braemar. Both were Mackerachers or M'Farquhars, that is Farquharsons, but each was best known by a name given to him on account of his character or appearance. The Athole man was known as Lonavey from the Gaelic *lonach* or greedy and *fiadh* deer, meaning that he was a dedicated deer hunter, while the Braemar Mackeracher was known as Mackeracher Ruadh on account of his red hair.

The two were kinsmen in some degree, and hunted either together or singly as it suited them, and there was keen rivalry between them regarding their skill as hunters. When in Athole, they frequently escaped the pursuit of legitimate forest rangers by making use of a secret cave, known only to themselves, and which baffled all those who searched for it. When pursued, it was observed that they invariably made for a certain rocky face and there they disappeared 'as though the earth had swallowed them up'. And so, for many years they hunted in safety, until one season the knowledge began to spread of an enormous stag with a magnificent head which was the coveted prize of every stalker in Athole and Braemar, and not least of Lonavey and Mackeracher Ruadh. Far and wide they searched, in glen and corrie and in every known haunt of deer, till one afternoon they spotted him and the stalk began. However, a stag of this size which has been the object of so many hunters has inevitably acquired a superior skill in self preservation, and the shades of evening found them further from their quarry than when the stalk began. Throwing themselves on the heather, each one vowed that he would shoot at no other stag until the one they had seen had fallen to one or other of them. At dawn they separated, each taking the path he thought would lead him to the stag.

For a whole week they searched, sometimes in sight of one another and sometimes alone, until, on the eighth morning, Lonavey heard a shot on the back of Cairn Righ and felt certain that his kinsman and rival had come up with the stag. With eager, excited steps he bounded over the shoulder of the hill and there, to his astonishment, he saw his friend and the stag in mortal conflict. Mackeracher Ruadh had been so near and so sure of his aim that, immediately on firing, he had thrown down his gun and, drawing his dirk, had rushed in to close quarters – all too soon as it proved.

As Lonavey shouted encouragement, Mackeracher Ruadh was pushed back by the infuriated stag and lost his footing on a heathery bank. As he fell, the stag gored him frightfully with its antlers, but at the same moment the dirk found its way into the heart of the huge creature which fell dead above him.

Lonavey, throwing off the stag, bent over his friend, who lay with his face deadly pale and still grasping in his right hand the bloodstained dirk. Tenderly raising him up, Lonavey anxiously enquired, 'Oh, Donald! Donald! has the stag hurt you?' Opening his eyes, Donald managed to whisper, 'Oh, Ian! Ian! I have killed the big stag, but the big stag has killed me!' Thus, in the moment of victory, fell Mackeracher Ruadh.

Lonavey, though now companionless, continued his old way of life, and now that he had no rival his reputation increased rather than diminished. At about this time, the Earl of Athole used to bring every summer a gang of mowers from England to cut and cure his meadow hay, as these men were more skilled in this than the Athole men of that time. After the haymaking, the earl gave a holiday to his men which included competitions of various kinds. Year after year, the Englishmen defeated the Athole men at shooting, and this angered the earl so that he demanded to know if there was no-one who could uphold the honour of his estate. He was told that there was one man, but that His Lordship would not care to ask him, and that, even if he did, it was doubtful if he would come. The earl at once guessed that Lonavey was the man and he promised that, if he would come to Athole and shoot, all old scores would be forgotten. Knowing the earl to be a man of his word, Lonavey arrived at the scene of the competition where, to their surprise and delight, the Englishmen saw that he had only one hand. (The punishment for poaching deer in those days was to cut off the left hand to make sure the poacher could never use the longbow again, and this barbarous act had been inflicted years before on Lonavey). Now, however, he had a matchlock gun and, using a rest which he planted in the ground at the moment of firing, he sent his shot nearer to the centre of the target than any of the other competitors and so secured victory for Athole.

He was presented with the prize, and the earl remarked that if he wanted to shoot deer on Athole he hoped he would not take too many. This was as good as saying that if he were not too *lonach* his activities would not be noticed.

But eventually another earl succeeded, and no quarter was shown to any poacher. Lonavey was found in the act of shooting a deer and, although he escaped, he knew it was just a matter of time before he was taken, and that imprisonment in Perth would be his certain fate. He went to his cave and left there his trusted gun and his dirk, and to make sure the former was preserved as far as possible, he filled the barrel with marrow oil from a deer. As he had feared, he was at last apprehended and imprisoned. At first, he thought he would soon be released for so trifling a matter as the killing of a deer, but as the weeks turned to months his spirits sank. He longed for the heights of Cairn Righ and Ben-y-Gloe, and one day, when walking in the walled enclosure of the prison, his sportsman's eye caught sight of a bird flying over the little space above, he exclaimed in Gaelic what might be translated thus:

> Had I my gun from Cairn Righ's height
> I'd break your wing and stop your flight.

Now there happened to be another Athole man in the prison with Lonavey, and this man asked how his gun could possibly be on Cairn Righ. Poor Lonavey, finding his companion knew much of the ground over which he used to hunt, found some consolation in talking of his past exploits, and eventually confided that his gun and dirk were in a secret cave known only to himself. He described how he had filled the barrel with oil, and how he hoped the gun would still be in good condition when he was released. He also explained that there was, in the roof of the cave, a small opening through which the sun could shine on only one day of the year, and that if it were a clear day at noon on the longest day, the sunlight would fall on his beloved gun. Eventually, his companion was released, but confinement to a man of Lonavey's habits was more than he could endure, and his companion had not long been home when word reached him of Lonavey's death. The story of the gun and the dirk spread and search was made for them for many a year. Generations came and went, and each one handed on to the next the story of Lonavey, the great hunter, and of the mysterious hidden cave where, at noon on midsummer day, the sun would shine on the gun and the dirk.

The story was a favourite one among the Straloch Farquharsons, and it is not surprising that it had an added fascination for a certain young man who lived two hundred years after Lonavey, for was his name not Ian Mackeracher or M'Farquhar, which in modern times is plain John Farquharson? And so, as young John grew up, he had this dream – might he not become a famous shot and bring down a deer in the forest of Athole? Might it even be that he was destined to discover the secret cave and the gun and the dirk of his hero? As so often happens in such matters, it was chance, pure chance, that made his dream come true and brought to light what the most patient search by gamekeepers, shepherds, poachers and fox-hunters had for generations failed to discover.

One day in the 1860s, Farquharson was out stalking in Athole forest, and had just brought down a stag when he saw three men approaching him at a great pace. He set off towards a rocky face with the three men in full pursuit. The ground was rough and stony, speed was impossible and capture seemed certain, but there was a chance that, if he could just get round the shoulder of the hill, he might be out of sight for a few minutes and be able to hide. Crouching behind a large boulder, he noticed in front of him an overhanging ledge of rock, beneath which was an opening. Quickly crawling under the ledge, he was astonished to find that there was a wide chimney-like opening above him. In this he could stand comfortably, but he knew that if his pursuers came close they would see his feet under the ledge. To prevent this, he began to grope about, feeling for some support to which he could cling, and so be able to draw up his legs. In doing so, he found an opening striking off at right angles to the chimney he was standing in, and leading horizontally into the hill.

Into this opening he quickly crawled, and, as the rocky mountain face carried no footprints, his pursuers were completely baffled. Soon Farquharson could hear their footsteps and their voices. They were certain that he could not have gone beyond where they could see in any direction. They examined the rocks all round with a running commentary of wonder and curses. At last, defeated and frustrated, they gave up and set off for home, one of them remarking that in his opinion the earth must have opened up and swallowed their quarry.

The moment Farquharson heard this remark, he remembered that these were the very words used by those who had pursued Lonavey. Trembling with excitement, he lit a match and discovered that he was indeed at the entrance of a large natural cave, about fourteen feet in length, twelve in breadth and eight feet high. At the far end, there appeared to be a rocky shelf about three feet above the level of the floor. After lighting a few more matches, he sat down in the darkness to think, but as he thought his eyes became accustomed to the darkness and he realised that there was, in fact, a dim light in the cave which came from what appeared to be an opening in the roof. His excitement returned, intensified and unbearable. Could this be the slit through which the sunlight came once a year to shine on the gun and the dirk? You or I would have rushed forward, striking matches with feverish haste, but not so Farquharson. He sat down again to think. Was this in fact the real Lonavey's cave? If so, was he the first to have entered it since the old poacher's death over two hundred years before? Was it indeed true that a gun and a dirk had been left here? Many had come to doubt the whole story, but if it were true then the gun and dirk must lie in the direction of the dim rays of light which seemed to go straight to the ledge he had observed. Striking another match, he advanced to the ledge and there lay *a gun and a dirk.*

He stood spellbound till the match burned his fingers. Then it was true! Another John Farquharson, living two hundred years before, had believed, like himself, that all God's creatures living in the wild belonged to all men, but with right but no might on his side he had been pursued by those with might but, as he thought, no right, and he had taken refuge in this very cave.

Once more he began to light matches, and looked with awe on the rust-eaten weapons that had lain for so long unseen by human eyes. Of the gun, only the metal parts remained and these were badly corroded. The wood of the stock was mere dust. The dirk, too, was almost eaten away by rust, but had obviously once been a formidable weapon. It was about sixteen inches long and had evidently been the point of a sword inserted into a wooden handle and secured with brass rivets.

Some days later, Farquharson reverently removed these relics and took them home; but their condition was so poor that they did not long survive, and the last mention we have of the gun barrel it was being used by his sister to poke the kitchen fire. *Sic transit gloria mundi!*

RECOVERING THE DEER

One day, while Farquharson was still in his teens, he set out for Ben-y-Gloe with a companion. Each carried a double-barrel fowling piece loaded with three buckshot on top of a round ball – a powerful and murderous load which was common in those days. Arriving, before sunrise, within a mile of Ben-y-Gloe, they spied

a herd of deer feeding on a grassy snow-covered slope beside a little hut used by a shepherd in the summer months. The stalk began and a hind was brought down, but it was now daylight and it was decided to return with a pony and remove it by night. It was hidden near the hut, and the two stalkers made their way home through the hills. There was a danger, however, that their tracks through the snow might have been detected, and a watch set over the deer. Three cold, wet nights followed, and it was thought that even if the hind had been found, the watchers would have given up their vigil.

On the fourth night, Farquharson and his friend returned with the pony. They reconnoitred the ground carefully with a telescope, but saw nothing to arouse their suspicion. However, when about three hundred yards from the hut, both became aware of the distinctive smell of peat smoke.

Obviously the hut was occupied, but it was just possible that it was not the gamekeeprs who were warming themselves with the shepherd's peats, and even if it were, they could not be keeping a watch on the deer unless they had it in the hut with them.

Mac crept closer, but soon returned with bad news. He had recognised the voice of one of the gamekeepers.

'We'll sit doon and hae a short rest,' he said, 'and a smoke and I'll tell you o' a plan I've fa'en on tae get the hind home wi's. When I was hark'nin' at the back o' the hut, a shooer o' sparks flew oot o' the lum heid which is nae owre nine feet heich. Aff I ran, thinkin' the roof had ta'en fire aboot the lum heid and that the wasps would be oot. So it came into my heid that if the concern had gone up in a blaze we would have had a fine chance to pack aff wi' the beast, the time they lads were thrang pittin' oot the fire. Noo, if you would pu' aff your boots wi' me an' tak' this box o' spunks, you'll easy get up to the lum frae the bank an' pit a lichted spunk tae the heathery stack roon aboot it, an' they half-fu' lads'll never dream but it was an accident, an' the hale concern's nae worth tuppence-ha'penny onyway.'

Farquharson at once agreed to the plan and set off with the box of matches. He crept cautiously forward and was soon close to the hut. There was great hilarity inside. Matchbox in hand, he mounted to the roof by the gavel wall and, with his ear close to the lum head, the first words he heard were, 'I expect some o' those Farquharsons will ring the bell directly.'

'Aye,' said a well-known voice, 'it was ower wet for them to turn oot earlier the nicht.'

'I defy them,' added a third voice which he recognised, 'tae pit a hand on the deer wi'out our kennin' o't.'

'Aha,' thought Farquharson, 'I would like to know how that can be.'

'We'd better be ready,' said the first speaker, 'hand me the bottle, Allie Mor.'

There was less smoke now as the fire was burning low, and as Farquharson heard the chink of the bottle on glass he took the chance of peering down the chimney which was, in fact, little more than a hole in the roof. He was reluctant to burn the shepherd's little shieling and, having heard one of the party say no-one could put a hand on the deer without their knowing of it, he guessed that they had it in the hut with them.

Determined to find out, he cautiously pushed his head further over the side of the chimney. Down below were the three jolly watchers, but no deer – only pots, bottles and cudgels lying about the floor. The glasses were filled again and one of the men, who was having a smoke, dropped his pipe-lid on the floor. As he stooped to pick it up, the man with the bottle suddenly spoke in a whisper, 'Lord, they're at the door noo lads, the chain's shakin'.'

'Maybe I touched the string,' said the other, 'when I was lookin' for my pipe-lid.'

Farquharson now saw that the chain which hung over the fire, normally to carry a pot or kettle, was being put to a very different use. It had been pulled slightly to one side, and attached to it was a string which stretched across the bothy and disappeared under the door. There was now an expectant silence in the hut, and all eyes were on the string. After a few moments, the bottle-holder spoke again. 'False alarm, lads, false alarm. The poachers have no' arrived yet.'

The tinkle of bottle on glass was resumed, and Farquharson became bolder. With his head in full view, he stared down the chimney and all became clear to him. The string was attached to the hind which had been brought to the door of the hut, and any attempt to remove it would have pulled the string and agitated the chain – a clever device which accounted for the confidence and high spirits of the three keepers.

After the false alarm the laughter and jokes began again. One remarked, 'We'd be a' richt noo if only we had a steak off yon fat hind.'

'Aye,' said another, 'and by my faith, if naebody comes by twa o'clock, I say we've watched lang enough and we'll hae a belly o't.'

He then made some joke and the third, a big fellow in a kilt, threw back his head and roared with laughter. His gaze was directed straight at the lum-hole, but, by a lucky chance, as he laughed he closed his eyes and Farquharson quickly withdrew his head. He climbed down from the roof just in time to see Mac approaching with the pony, and ran forward to stop him.

'Mercy! What kept you?' asked Mac in an angry voice. 'I made sure they had a haud o' ye when I saw nae spark o' a fire, and I was just on my way to buy ye aff wi' a keg o' whisky!'

He was at once in a good humour again when Farquharson explained what he had seen, and they soon had a plan to secure the hind. Mac was to hold the pony while Farquharson crept forward to the hind where the keepers had hidden it. The string was tied to a foreleg, and the problem was to remove it without the slightest movement. He thrust his stick into the ground beside the string, then, pressing the string to the staff with his thumb so as to maintain the same tension, he cut it from the hind and wound it round the staff. This done, it was only a moment's work to get the hind on his back and make his way to the pony. Soon the hind was securely on its back, and they were on their way down Glenfernate. On the way, they met a lad carrying provisions to the watchers in the hut. He was evidently astonished to see the hind on the pony's back, and hurried on to report this to the gamekeeprs who were quickly sobered when they discovered that the hind had been transformed into a thin hazel stick. Early next morning, they tracked the pony down the glen as far as the main road, but here the trail ended. Meeting Mac next morning, Farquharson remarked that it was a pity they had even got his stick, but Mac replied, 'The spiders that got your stick lost the flies their web was spread for.'

A DAY WITH JOHN FARQUHARSON

You will by now realise that, for John Farquharson, legitimate shooting lacked the challenge and excitement of poaching, and here is another story which demonstrates this.

One of his Scottish friends had a good position in South Wales, where he was the undisputed champion pigeon shot of the district. This friend, although he had abundant shooting in Wales, was eagerly looking forward to his annual holiday at the end of October, when he hoped to have a day or two among the grouse of his native hills. He knew that these would provide sport incomparably superior to that available in the south, and he was not disappointed.

When he and Farquharson set out on the first day, it was apparent that the birds were strong and wild, testing even the skill of these two fine sportsmen. Something else was apparent too, and that was the fierce but friendly rivalry between the two – Farquharson relying on his long-standing reputation, and his friend on his recent successes in pigeon shooting. Each claimed to be the better shot and, to settle the matter, a match was arranged for the next day, with a mutual friend as umpire. The competitors were to walk in a straight line one hundred yards apart, and were to shoot for six hours. The birds were as wild as ever and, when the first three hours brought lunch, the bags were light.

After lunch, the second three hours began, and John Farquharson always

John Farquharson

looked back on this as one of the most trying ordeals he ever endured. The pace was fast, the competition intense, and the birds, being wild, rose so far out that long shots were the order of the day. Adding to the excitement was the probability that a gamekeeper or two might appear at any moment with the threat of a fine or imprisonment, and it is certain that these guardians of the moors missed a rare opportunity that afternoon, for in the last hour neither man would have turned aside a yard to avoid capture if it meant losing the match.

As the light began to fade the umpire called, 'Time's up!' and the three drew together to count the birds. His friend asked Farquharson what his bag was and he replied, 'Twenty-one birds.'

The friend had nineteen and the umpire, who had also been shooting, had thirteen. But, of course, the birds had to be counted by the umpire, and each man emptied his bag beside a small stream, counting out his birds as he did so. The friend laid his out in a row and there were nineteen, but when Farquharson's were laid out there were only eighteen.

'Where are your twenty-one birds?' asked the umpire.

'There before you,' was the reply.

'No, there are only eighteen – see for yourself.'

Farquharson did so, and to his dismay found only eighteen, but, being confident he had taken twenty-one out of the bag and placed them in a heap, he quite naturally concluded that either his rival or the umpire had removed three for a joke. Both denied this and made it quite plain that they believed there had never been more than eighteen. Farquharson was ordered to admit defeat and pay the wager, but, so sure was he that a trick had been played on him, that he replaced the birds in his bag, swung this onto his back and strode away, too angry to speak. As he did so, his foot sank through the soft moss where he had emptied the grouse out of his bag. Withdrawing his foot and examining the hole, what should he see but feathers! In an instant the bag was on the ground, and thrusting in his arm he pulled out a grouse.

'That makes it a tie, at any rate,' he said, as he reached into the hole again. 'And that one wins the match!' as he pulled out another. Still he was sure there should be twenty-one; but he could feel no more in the hole so, taking the ramrod of his gun, he uncovered the screw at the end and thrust it right to the bottom of the hole and in triumph brought out the last bird.

Those who know the Highland hills will have noticed that small streams will often flow underground for part of their course, peeping out and disappearing in the most unexpected manner. These little streams often change course, and in doing so the ground is left undermined with only a thin crust of moss covering the old stream bed. It was into one of these that Farquharson's grouse had fallen, and when this was understood good humour once more prevailed.

They gathered up the grouse and set off to meet the trap which had been ordered to meet them in a neighbouring glen; but here bad news awaited them. Their trusty driver reported that their shooting had been heard and that every road home was now watched. It was even suspected that he himself was going to meet the poachers, and particular note had been made of the appearance of his horse and dogcart, so as to waylay it on the return journey.

A council of war was held, and, although no whisky had been drunk during the match, the driver had brought a good supply for the return journey and now a stiff dram was had by all. Various plans were discussed and rejected. Another dram went round, and under its strengthening influence the boldest plan of all was decided upon. They would run the blockade with a brave and glorious game of bluff; but to shorten the odds a few preparations would have to be made.

The gamekeepers had taken note of a turnout with no lights, but the driver now produced two lamps which he proceeded to light. His wife, too, had entered into the spirit of the adventure and produced several white hats to replace the usual dark shooting caps. The bottle went round again, and they were all in fine fettle to run the blockade when Farquharson noticed that the horse had no white on its face. He knew the gamekeepers would have noted this fact so, to complete the disguise, he fixed a white handkerchief between the noseband and the browband of the bridle, and in an instant gave the obliging animal a beautiful white blaze.

So far, so good – the watchers were expecting an unlit dog-cart drawn by a horse with a dark face and occupied by the driver and three men in dark caps. What they would see was a well-lit vehicle drawn by a horse with a white face and occupied by three men in white hats. They were also expecting three silent, suspicious poachers sneaking as quietly down the glen as possible; but our three jolly sportsmen changed all that. The driver reported that a meeting of some sort had taken place in the village that evening, and that some high-spirited revellers were on their way home.

Why not join them?

Warmed by the whisky, the three friends loudly told stories and jokes. They roared with laughter, they argued and shouted and sang, and all the danger spots were passed in a storm of good cheer. At last there was only one left, and as no watchers had been seen so far they were sure to be on this narrow bridge. As they approached, the trio could see a party of gamekeepers and policemen gathered by the bridge. They burst into song:

> For we are jolly good fellows,
> For we are jolly good fellows,
> For we are jolly good fellows,
>   Which nobody can deny!

The harmony might not have been perfect, but the enthusiasm of the singers was not in doubt. Carried away by the infectious merriment, the keepers and policemen gave an answering wave and called out, 'Hurrah, lads!' and the party dashed past.

Once out of danger the singing and shouting just gave way to uncontrollable laughter.

GLENSHEE GAMEKEEPERS OUTWITTED

Farquharson and a friend were one day returning from a day's shooting in Glenshee. Sport had been good and the bags were heavy as they set off for home. The route chosen meant crossing the Shee where there is a high bank on the north side, but when they arrived there the river was in flood and unfordable. They were about to move downstream when they spotted two gamekeepers. Farquharson quickly gave his gun and bag to his companion and told him to go down to the water's edge in the shelter of the high bank, while he would keep the gamekeepers occupied till the other could turn another promontary further down. While his companion was making the best speed possible downstream, he stood up in full view and started upstream, while apparently signalling to his friends to do the same.

This made the keepers also turn upstream, and Farquharson, going down the face of the bank, quickly turned his coat and cap, which were reversible, grey on one side and blue on the other, took out a newspaper and was quietly reading from it when the gamekeepers came down on him.

'Did ye see whaur yon twa men gaid, sir?' said one.
'Two men,' said Farquharson leisurely. 'Had they a dog?'
'Yes.'
'Bags on their backs?'
'Yes.'
'Guns?'
'Yes.'
'Well, you can easily see they're not here,' said Farquharson coolly as he settled down to read again. Meanwhile his comrade was well out of sight and the game-keepers set off upstream as fast as they could, one of them remarking that that was the way the man in the grey coat had gone. As they disappeared, the man in the blue coat walked quietly off to join his companion.

A WONDERFUL DREAM

My last story about John Farquharson is the strangest of all, and I will leave you to make of it what you will. From what I have heard and read about that remark-able man, I believe it is impossible that he invented or imagined it.

About the year 1870, Farquharson and his brother Archie set out to have two days stalking along the boundary between Athole and Braemar forests. As they were ascending the hills to the north of Glenshee about two hours before daylight, there came on a heavy downpour of rain mixed with sleet. They were making for a shepherd's hut which they expected to find unoccupied at that time of year – the beginning of October. Before reaching it, Farquharson sprained one of his feet, which became very swollen and painful. On reaching the hut, which was unoccupied as they had expected, an examination of the foot showed that he would not be able to move for a day at least. While he remained in the hut doctoring his foot and drying his clothes by a peat fire, Archie took a turn round to look for deer, but saw none that day.

Next morning, the foot was still somewhat stiff and sore, and again Archie set off alone.

Farquharson lay down to ease his foot, and in a little while dozed off to sleep. As his waking thoughts were all of deerstalking, it is not surprising that in his dreams he and Archie were soon engaged in creeping stealthily down a corrie a little south from Lochnanean. As they advanced, more and more of the corrie came in sight, but nothing in it. They began to lose heart, but something impelled Farquharson on and on, until they both fancied there was no nook left for a deer to hide in. Still Farquharson would not turn, and was wondering how he might descend a little further, when all at once, a stag arose which had been invisible so long as he lay beneath them, turned round and lay down again, becoming lost to view behind a rocky spur. They must get up to that spur to get a shot, and the intervening ground was rough and stony. They both took off their boots and crept forward till they could see over the rocky spur. There he lay, with the back of his head towards them. Inch by inch, they raised their rifles and fired simultaneously, both bullets entering the back of his head within an inch of each other. So vivid was the whole thing that when Farquharson awoke he was impatient for Archie to come back, and, putting on his boots, he felt the lame foot was good for a few miles stalking with a deer in front.

Archie soon returned, much dispirited, having seen only one stag which saw him first and made off. This stag was a little lame on a foreleg, which probably accounted for his being alone. Things, in Archie's opinion, had a gloomy look, as they must return this night, and the trap that was ordered to meet them seemed likely to return empty, as far as deer were concerned. As for Farquharson, when he heard of the stag, he enquired what direction he had taken, and on hearing that it had crossed into Glentaitneach, he had no doubt that it was on its way to meet its fate, as that glen lay between them and the corrie where they shot the stag – in his dream. He now told the particulars of his dream to Archie, who listened patiently but laughed at the idea of seeing the dream fulfilled.

However, as there was nothing else that seemed more hopeful, he consented to lead Farquharson to where the stag disappeared, in the faint hope that they might be able to track it to some spot where a stalk might be possible.

In a short time, they were on the trail, but found it so difficult that in just under two hours they had gone less than a mile. By this time, however, they saw that the trail was in the direction of the corrie of the dream, and Farquharson's hopes revived again. To follow on was useless, as the stag would be careful that no-one came on him in his rear. They therefore decided to make a long circuit and come in on him from the head of the corrie.

Freed from the trouble of tracking the stag on the soft ground, they made good progress and soon came onto high ground, from which in a little they began to see the lower end of the corrie. Cautiously they descended on it, but with very different feelings. The more Archie saw of the corrie, the more dispirited he became, while as each successive part of it came into Farquharson's view his spirits rose higher, for he recognised in every detail the corrie of his dream. At last, they came to where, in his dream, it seemed they saw every corner where a deer could hide. Here Archie, who had been placing far more reliance on his telescope and his instincts as a stalker than on the dream, after a careful look round, shut his telescope and, with a contemptuous gesture, said in a low voice, 'What about your precious dream now?'

Hardly, however, were the words out of his mouth, when Farquharson seized him by the arm and pointed out the horns of a stag which had stood up as in his dream. Everything followed as already described in his dream. After they fired, Farquharson sent Archie back for their boots, and by the time he reached the stag, he was standing with two of his fingers in the bullet holes, asking triumphantly, 'What do you think of my dream now?'

He was a fine large stag with one cloot of a forefoot broken, and proved a heavy burden when the best of him was divided between them.

Doubtless many will say that the above dream and its fulfilment is more imaginary than real. Yet it is strictly true. Farquharson's brother, who, to begin with, regarded the story of the dream as a joke, was more impressed with its fulfilment than he was. Had Farquharson merely said at first that he had dreamed of a stalk, without giving the details, and after the stalk had said everything had occurred according to his dream, his brother would still have laughed at him; but as he had given the particulars before he had set out, exactly as they afterwards took place, there was no room for doubting.

I have given you this story almost exactly in the words of William M'Combie Smith, but I would just add that, from the description of the corrie, both in the dream and afterwards in the stalk, I have no doubt that it is the Glascorrie Bheag which I know well, and where I too have shot more than one stag. The whole tale has to me the ring of absolute truth.

15 *An Officer and a Gentleman*

This chapter is about two Highland officers who fought with distinction in Europe and afterwards in the American War of Independence. It was in this latter sad and unnecessary struggle that both earned the undying respect of the American people by their chivalrous conduct which, in the case of Patrick Ferguson, may well have changed the course of American history.

JOHN SMALL was the third son of Patrick Small who received the lands of Leanoch in Glenshee from his father (also Patrick), fourth laird of Dirnanean.

Born in Strathardle in 1730 (according to the Kirkmichael Parish Register he was baptised on 2nd December of that year), Small, like many of his countrymen at that time, began his military career with the Scots Brigade in Holland, being appointed a 2nd lieutenant in the Earl of Drumlanrig's Regiment when it was raised for the service of the States General in 1747. It was not, however, until 1756 that he obtained a commission in the British Army, when he became a lieutenant in the Black Watch (42nd) just before its departure for America.

He took part in all the campaigns in which this regiment was engaged from 1756 until 1763, including the first disastrous attack on Fort Ticonderoga in 1758, and later served with General Amherst's successful expedition to Lake Champlain which resulted in the surrender of Fort Ticonderoga (his dirk is on display in the museum there) and ended with the capture of Montreal and the final expulsion of the French from Canada. After the surrender of Montreal, he was sent in charge of French prisoners to New York, and it was said by a brother officer that General Amherst had great confidence in him, and frequently employed him 'on particular services'. Two years later, he was present at the capture of Martinique and Havana and was promoted captain.

At the peace of 1763, Small was placed on half-pay but, according to General Stewart, he was almost immediately restored to the full-pay list of the North British Fusiliers (21st), and when in 1767 the Black Watch left for Europe, most of the men of that regiment who had volunteered to stay in America joined the Fusiliers in order to serve under an officer who was 'deservedly popular' with them.

It was probably during the interval of peace between the Seven Years War and the war with the American colonies (as they then were), that Small began to acquire a substantial property in Nova Scotia and interest himself in local politics. He was town-major of Boston at the time of the outbreak of the War of Independence and, as we shall see, he had some close friends among the American people.

He was present as a brigade major at the Battle of Bunker's Hill on 17th June 1775, and is described as landing some 400 marines to take part in the action.

Bunker's Hill is situated on a small peninsula separated by a narrow stretch of water from the town of Boston, and on the night of 16th June the Americans occupied and fortified the top of the adjacent Breed's Hill. The Military Governor of Massachusetts, General Thomas Gage, decided on a show of force and, in full view of the watching inhabitants of Boston, he ordered a direct frontal attack on the American positions.

On the hot afternoon of 17th, General Howe, under Gage's orders, drew up his men and made them a speech.

'You must drive these farmers from the hill, or it will be impossible for us to remain in Boston. But I shall not desire any of you to advance a single step beyond where I am at the head of your line.'

In three lines the Redcoats, or 'lobsters' as they were known by the local people, advanced slowly towards the top of the hill, while the whole of Boston turned out to watch what promised to be the most thrilling spectacle of their lives.

At 100 yards from the trenches there was not a sound, but at 50 yards a hail of bullets and buckshot from ancient hunting guns smote the attackers. Many fell, and there was shouting and curses, but Howe, his white silk breeches splashed with blood, rallied his men. They advanced again, but were scattered by a second volley and driven back to the boats. Howe's reputation was at stake and he knew that ammunition was running short on the hilltop. He ordered a third assault, this time in column and not in line.

Leading one of the columns was John Small, and on reaching the American positions the first thing he saw was his friend, the American General Warren, lying wounded on the ground. He rushed forward and, seizing the musket of the leading British soldier, was just in time to prevent his friend from being bayonetted. Sadly, I must tell you that William Warren died from his wounds, but John Small's attempt to save him so vividly captured the imagination and gratitude of the American people that after the war their new Government commissioned a painting of the scene by their foremost artist, Colonel Trumbull. This famous painting now hangs in the art gallery at Yale University, and when I went to see it and explained that the central figure was an ancestor of mine, I was given a fine reproduction.

Small saw further action throughout the remainder of the war, but in 1784 hostilities were at an end and his battalion was disbanded at Windsor in Nova Scotia.

Now once more on half-pay, he returned home, but in 1790 he was promoted Colonel, and three years later was appointed Lieutenant Governor of Guernsey, an important post as by this time Britain was once more at war with France. It was in June 1794, during the period of Small's Governorship, that Sir James de Saumarez, though engaged by a French squadron, brought the *Crescent* and the *Druid* into safe anchorage off Guernsey, through a narrow and dangerous channel previously thought to be impassable by a warship – a manoeuvre watched with breathless excitement by all on the island. Small presented a medal to John Breton, the Guernsey pilot who brought in the *Crescent*, and not only published

The Battle of Bunker's Hill, by Colonel Trumbull (Yale University)

a general order expressing his appreciation of the masterly skill and seamanship of Sir James de Saumarez and his men, but, with characteristic kindness, wrote off at once to bring their services to the notice of the Admiralty.

In 1794 Small became a Major-General, and, on 17th March 1796, he died in Guernsey and is buried in the church in St Peter Port.

Perhaps the most eloquent tribute to this brave, kind and generous man comes from the pen of General Stewart of Garth who wrote, 'No chief of former days ever more firmly secured the attachment of his clan, and no chief certainly ever deserved it better. With an enthusiastic and almost romantic love of his country and countrymen, it seemed as if the principal object of his life had been to serve them and promote their prosperity. Equally brave in leading them in the field and kind, just and conciliating in quarters, they would indeed have been ungrateful if they had regarded him otherwise than they did'.

An actor whom Small befriended in Guernsey told of the General's kindness to him and various other French emigrants, adding that, 'His heart was an unfathomed depth of benevolence'.

An inscription on the back of the medallion illustrated here records that it is 'a very strong likeness of as worthy a man as ever was born'.

PATRICK FERGUSON was not a Glenshee man, but he did come from just 'over the hill' as we say in the Glen, and he has always been a hero of mine. Since a very early age – ten or thereabouts – rifle shooting in all its forms has fascinated me, and I have competed with varying degrees of success at school, at university, at Bisley and among the Perthshire hills. It is no wonder, therefore, that I have always admired this remarkable man – inventor of a breech-loading rifle 100 years before it was introduced into the British Army, and one of the most brilliant shots of his time.

He was born in 1744, the second son of James Ferguson of Pitfour and his wife Anne Murray, daughter of the fourth Lord Elibank, and we have a delightful description of him from Dr Marianne Gilchrist who writes, 'Pattie, as his family called him, was extremely slender – he often joked about being nothing but bone – and not very tall. But his features were handsome, slightly elfin-looking. His personal letters reveal him as being a gentle yet fun-loving young man with great wit and charm. He was intelligent, sensitive, honourable and remarkably courageous; flirtatious too when he had time! An articulate and expressive writer, it is a singular tragedy that he did not live to write his memoirs'.

He was taught fortification, gunnery and other military skills at an academy in London, and on 12th July 1759, before his fifteenth birthday, he was appointed Cornet in the Royal North British Dragoons, or Scots Greys. He served with

Patrick Ferguson

them in Germany in the Seven Years War, but fell seriously ill with an infected leg. Rather unwillingly, he returned home and spent the next few years with the Grey's Light Troop in various parts of Britain. Then, on 1st September 1768, a company was purchased for him in the 70th Foot in the West Indies. He remained with this regiment for some time and took part in the suppression of a negro rising in Tobago, but eventually returned home again.

He was exhausted, but a turning point had been reached in his career. At the outbreak of the American War of Independence in 1775, the boasted skill of the American marksmen directed his attention to the improvement of military firearms, and he set about designing a revolutionary new breech-loading rifle for which he obtained a patent on 2nd December 1776. The Patent Office lists 'Various improvements upon firearms whereby they are loaded with more ease, safety and expedition, fire with more certainty and possess other advantages'.

It is true that some of the principles had been tried before, in particular by a Frenchman, Chaumette, in the design of sporting guns, but 'had never been seriously applied to purposes of public utility'.

The patent covers several types of breech-action. In the first, which Ferguson appears to have adopted, the breech is closed by a vertical screw-plug which is lowered to allow the introduction of the ball, followed by the cartridge or charge. Special arrangements are provided against fouling of the screw-plug and accumulation of gas in the breech. A second plan, said to be particularly suitable for artillery, was to close the breech with a 'perpendicular or horizontal turnplate'. A third provided for the closing of the breech wth a sliding transverse bar.

The use of a sliding backsight, adjustable to any range, was also included in the patent, and so was a new and peculiar mode of rifling, in which the grooves were to be made of exaggerated width as compared to the 'lands' between them, the idea being that fouling of the bore and 'stripping' of the bullet in its passage down the barrel would be prevented.

The resulting weapon was, as I have said, 100 years ahead of its time and was more accurate at 500 yards than the muzzle-loading service weapon (which averaged scarcely one shot a minute) was at 100 yards. There was nothing like it in the world and its inventor was a genius, but Patrick Ferguson's skills did not end with the development of his new rifle – in its use too he was in a class of his own.

At Woolwich, in June 1776, before a crowd of distinguished officers, we are told that, 'under disadvantages of heavy rain and a high wind, he did the four following things, none of which had ever been accomplished with any kind of small arms, viz:

1. He fired during four or five minutes at a target 200 yards distant, at the rate of four shots a minute.
2. He fired six shots in one minute.
3. He fired four shots a minute, advancing at the same time at the rate of four miles an hour.
4. He poured a bottle of water into the barrel and pan of the piece when loaded, so as to wet every grain of the powder, and in less than half a minute fired as well as ever with her without extracting the ball. He also hit the target at 100 yards lying on his back on the ground,* and, notwithstanding the unequalness of the wind and the wetness of the weather, only missed the target three times during the whole course of the experiment'.

I have described the Ferguson rifle in detail and also its inventor's supreme skill as a marksman so that you will undertsand fully the significance of the dramatic events which follow.

Ferguson was sent back to America – his regiment was then at Halifax – and he was permitted to form a corps of riflemen out of volunteers from regiments in America. This little green-clad company of 100 men served first in New Jersey and then, in August 1777, sailed for Chesapeake to take part in General Howe's campaign to capture Philadelphia. Howe was impressed with their performance and promised that the little corps would be increased; but this was not to be.

Washington, whose men were by now better trained and, thanks to the French, better equipped, decided to block Howe's advance at Brandywine Creek. As this creek could only be forded in a few places, it was a good defensive position and Howe decided on a bold outflanking movement. He sent Lord Cornwallis and 12,500 men off upstream to come down on the Americans' right. Meanwhile, another column under General Knyphausen was ordered to advance towards the centre of the American line at Chad's Ford. They were a fairly easy target for Washington's sharpshooters, and the scene is vividly described in a letter dictated by Patrick Ferguson (in the National Library of Scotland):

While Knyphausen was forming the line within a mile of the Rebell camp to wait for G Howe's attack, their Rifle men were picking off our men very fast by random shots from a wood some hundred yards in front as it is easy to do execution upon such large objects. I had only twenty men with me (a few having been disabled by the enemy, the rest from fatigue) who however proved sufficient, for my lads first dislodged them from the skirts of the wood and then drove them from a breastwork within it, after which,

---

* When John Farquharson was told of this one hundred years later, he is quoted as saying, 'Solomon was right after all, there's nothing new under the sun'.

our purpose being answered, we lay down at the further skirt of the wood, not necessarily to provoke an attack being so few without support. We had not lyn long when a Rebell officer remarkable by a Huzzar dress passed towards our army within 100 yards of my right flank, not perceiving us – he was followed by another dressed in dark green or blue, mounted on a very good bay horse with a remarkable large high cocked hat. I ordered three good shots to steal near them and fire at them but the idea disgusted me and I recalled them. The Huzzar in returning made a circuit but the other passed within 100 yards of us upon which I advanced from the wood towards him. Upon my calling he stopd but, after looking at me, proceeded. I again drew his attention and made signs to him to stop, levelling my piece at him, but he slowly continued his way. As I was within that distance at which in the quickest firing I have seldom missed a sheet of paper and could have lodged half a dozen of balls in or about him before he was out of my reach I had only to determine, but it was not pleasant to fire at the back of an unoffending individual who was acquiting himself very coolly of his duty, so I let him alone. The day after I had just been telling this story to some wounded officers who lay in the same room with me when one of our surgeons who had been dressing the wounded Rebell Officers came in and told us that they had been informing him that Genl Washington was all the morning with the Light Troops generally in their front and only attended by a French officer in a Huzzar dress, he himself mounted and dressed as above described. The oddness of their dress had puzzled me and made me take notice of it. I am not sorry that I did not know all the time who it was.

(Scribe's note: 'further this deponent saith not, as his bones were broke a few minutes after'.)

This letter was dictated by Patrick Ferguson for, a few minutes after the events he describes, he was himself wounded, a ball shattering his right elbow. For eight months he remained in hospital in Philadelphia, undergoing numerous painful operations to remove bone splinters. In letters home, dictated or written with his left hand, he joked bravely about his plight and whether or not his arm should be amputated. In the end he kept it but was permanently crippled.

During this long absence his little company was disbanded and its rifles returned to store. The disappointment and the wound might have crushed a lesser man, but Pattie was determined to remain a soldier. He taught himself to fence and shoot with his left hand and, by the autumn of 1778, was leading daring raids such as that against the privateer base at Little Egg Harbor in New Jersey.

A year later, he was commissioned Major in Fraser's Highlanders (71st) and posted south for the campaign in the Carolinas where, on October 7th 1780, he fought his last battle. Surrounded by a superior force on King's Mountain, he was shot from his horse as he rallied his men. It is said that he died with eight bullets in his frail body.

He was buried under a cairn of stones on the battlefield, and his grave is tended by the Rangers of the King's Mountain National Military Park.

16 Some Notes from the Game Book

Red Grouse above Finegand.

Although we know much of the history of the Mackenzies we would know even more were it not for Uncle Mac's fondness for cigars and after dinner 'toddy'.

One evening he was studying a box of papers which lay open on his knee. He dozed off, the lighted cigar fell from his lips into the box and it was only the smell of the burning papers which woke him.

However, to make up in some measure for this accident, he kept, from 1869 till his death, a fascinating and detailed Game Book which was continued into a second volume by his nephew Billy. Together, these two books cover nearly one hundred years of life and sport at Finegand.

Most of the entries will be of interest only to the family, but here are just a few little cameos of life at Finegand a hundred years ago.

Game was plentiful, the weather for the most part appalling, and the family quite astonishingly hardy and fit. Which of our feeble generation would contemplate catching a hundred trout in the pouring rain or walking seventeen miles over the Cairnwell on a Sunday afternoon to have tea in Braemar? But then, would we, could we, drink 72 bottles of whisky and sherry and 96 pints of champagne in a month?

1871
This year J. W. Jeffcock on Glenquaich killed to his own gun and over one brace of dogs, running them singly, on 12th August 114 Brace Grouse, on 14th August 112 Brace Grouse.

1872
August 27th Colin and Kirke walked to Dirnanean to dine [six miles each way over a hill track].

August 28th Wet day. Kirke killed 4 dozen trout in the Shee.

August 29th Wet day. Colin, Kirke and Capt Clark fished Loch Baine. Rained most of the day. Killed 8 dozen and 7 trout.

1876

August 21st Kirke and Charlie fished from 10 to 12 in the loch and killed 28 fine trout, after which with M'Donald they killed 33 brace grouse.

1877

August 11th This being Minnie's first visit to the Glen, Colin drove us up in an open carriage and four through pouring rain which prevented her from seeing the beauties of the Glen.

August 13th Fine Mor'g. Started 9 am. Minnie started like a four-year-old, full of vigour and pluck and walked the whole day step by step with the guns, and returned at 6pm nearly as fresh as when she started. She consumed half a bottle of champagne and an immense number of nips of mountain dew and an enormous dinner at night, winding up at 10 pm with a stiff tumbler of toddy.

1881

August 12th Fine day but bitterly cold with a strong north wind blowing all day. Mac and Harry on Finegand, Colin and Kirke on Corrydon. Bag 65 brace and some extras. Minnie and Emma walked the hill all day and took very kindly to the whisky.

1883

August 12th The parcel post has commenced and will carry two brace of grouse to any destination for 1/– and a man to Blairgowrie for 3/– !

1885

August 13th This morning opened with a gale of wind and the hills thick with snow.

1888

August 12th All went to the Spital Kirk where for the first time a harmonium (the gift of Mr and Mrs Alexander Mackenzie Smith) was used in the service. Mr Crawford preached a very appropriate sermon on the use of instrumental music in public places of worship of all ages, and the people seemed well pleased with the addition to the Kirk.

1892

Wine ordered – Champagne 3 doz quts and 2 doz pints, 3 doz whisky and 2 bottles brandy, 3 doz sherry and 1 hamper pollonaris.

1910

August 29th Found the river in flood and over its banks. Higher than even Sandy can remember. Polgorm cottage surrounded and had to pull down the stye to rescue the pig.

September 4th Mabel, Susan and Victoria Hicks Beach and Gilbert went to the Kirk and then walked over the hill to Braemar for tea at the Fife Arms.

1911

August 11th Party met at Blairgowrie and motored up in Philip's Panhard car which he had sent up by sea to Dundee and intends to leave for annual use at Finegand.

August 25th All went to Glenisla Games in Philip's Panhard motor. Gearbox broke down coming home. Passengers walked home and the car was driven home backwards.

1932

September 4th A motor bus ran away at the Lair Brae and leapt 20 feet into a field. No-one much hurt.

1933

August 19th Record Bag 425 grouse.

1944

August 4th [Extracts from the *Blairgowrie Advertiser*] On 4th August Mrs Robertson, Corrydon Lodge, Glenshee, reached her 100th birthday. At the request of Colonel Mackenzie Smith, a flagpole was erected and a Union Jack unfurled at 6 am, the beginning of a memorable day ... Like other aged persons, Mrs Robertson likes to recall the days that are gone. She remembers the first minister of Cray, the Rev. William Brown, who loved to be out in a thunderstorm at night. He would walk up and down one of the fields near his house, listening to the crack and rumble of the thunder. Asked why he indulged in this practice, he said he liked to listen to the voice of God in the thunder. She also remembers the second minister, the Rev. James Robertson, and how he divided his sermon every Sunday into two parts – one addressed to the saved and the other to the unsaved, and how his address to the latter was so affecting in its pleading appeal for repentance that many of the people wept.

17 *Poetry and Song*

The poetry and song of Scotland reflect above all else the fierce pride of the Highlander and his passionate love of home and country, but there is also, all through it, a thread of sadness which tells of lost battles and separation from all that is loved.

The examples I have chosen are not all about Glenshee, but all, I think, have their echoes in the lives of its people, and so are included here.

The first is one of the most stirring poems of Sir Walter Scott. I learned it at school in Perthshire and have remembered it in all my travels:

PATRIOTISM

Breathes there the man with soul so dead,
Who never to himself hath said,
'This is my own, my native land!'
Whose heart hath ne'er within him burn'd
As home his footsteps he hath turn'd
From wandering on a foreign strand?
If such there be, go mark him well.
For him no Minstrel raptures swell;
High though his titles, proud his name,
Boundless his wealth as wish can claim;
Despite those titles, power and pelf,
The wretch, concentred all in self,
Living, shall forfeit fair renown,
And, doubly dying, shall go down
To the vile dust from whence he sprung,
Unwept, unhonour'd, and unsung.

When I returned to Finegand there were some who said, 'After years in the Navy and at College, won't you be lonely in the Glen?' The answer, quite simply, was, 'No, why should I be?'

> To sit on rocks, to muse o'er flood and fell;   Lord Byron 1788–1824
> To slowly trace the forest's shady scene,
> Where things that own not man's dominion dwell,
> And mortal foot hath ne'er or rarely been!
> To climb the trackless mountain all unseen,
> With the wild flock, that never need a fold;
> Alone o'er steeps and foaming falls to lean;
> This is not solitude; 'tis but to hold
> Converse with Nature's charms,
> And view her stores unrolled.

The next two delightful little poems are typically English, but are here because they idealise the life of the shepherd which, after all, is what the Mackenzies were for so many generations and what I was myself when I lived in the Glen:

THE WAKENING

John Attye's *First Book of Airs*, 1622

On a time the amorous Silvy
Said to her shepherd, 'Sweet, how do ye?
Kiss me this once and then God be wi' ye,
My sweetest dear!
Kiss me this once and then God be wi' ye,
For now the morning draweth near.'

With that, her fairest bosom showing,
Op'ning her lips, rich perfumes blowing,
She said, 'Now kiss me and be going,
My sweetest dear!
Kiss me this once and then be going,
For now the morning draweth near.'

With that the shepherd waked from sleeping,
And spying where the day was peeping,
He said, 'Now take my soul in keeping,
My sweetest dear!
Kiss me and take my soul in keeping,
Since I must go, now day is near.'

THE PASSIONATE SHEPHERD TO HIS LOVE

Christopher Marlowe, 1564–1593

Come live with me and be my love,
And we will all the pleasures prove
That hills and valleys, dales and fields,
Or woods or steepy mountain yields.

And we will sit upon the rocks,
And see the shepherds feed their flocks
By shallow rivers, to whose falls
Melodious birds sing madrigals.

And I will make thee beds of roses
And a thousand fragrant posies;
A cap of flowers, and a kirtle
Embroider'd all with leaves of myrtle.

A gown made of the finest wool
Which from our pretty lambs we pull;
Fair-lined slippers for the cold,
With buckles of the finest gold.

A belt of straw and ivy-buds
With coral clasps and amber studs;
And if these pleasures may thee move,
Come live with me and be my love.

The shepherd swains shall dance and sing
For thy delight each May morning;
If these delights thy mind may move,
Then live with me and be my love.

Though there were undoubtedly idyllic times for the Highland shepherd, specially in the summer, it was not always so. The Battle of Flodden Field in 1514 was one of the greatest disasters in Scottish history, and there was scarcely a glen in the Highlands which did not mourn for the young men who never came home. Jane Elliot's lament gives a heart-breaking picture of the empty lives of those who remained, and hearing this mournful dirge on the pipes one cannot escape a feeling of infinite sadness.

A LAMENT FOR FLODDEN   Jane Elliot, 1727–1805

I've heard them lilting at our ewe-milking,
Lasses a' lilting before the dawn o' day;
But now they are all moaning on ilka green loaning –
The Flowers of the Forest are a' wede away.

At bughts, in the morning, nae blythe lads are scorning,
Lasses are lonely and dowie and wae;
Nae daffing, nae gabbing, but sighing and sabbing,
Ilka ane lifts her leglin and hies her away.
In hairst, at the shearing, nae youths now are jeering,
Bandsters are lyart, and runkled and gray;
At fair or at preaching, nae wooing, nae fleeching –.
The Flowers of the Forest are a' wede away.

At e'en, in the gloaming, nae swankies are roaming
'Bout stacks wi' the lasses at bogle to play;
But ilka ane sits eerie, lamenting her dearie –
The Flowers of the Forest are a' wede away.

Dool and wae for the order sent our lads to the Border!
The English, for ance, by guile wan the day;
The Flowers of the Forest, that fought aye the foremost,
The prime of our land, lie cauld in the clay.

We'll hear nae mair lilting at our ewe-milking;
Women and bairns are heartless and wae;
Sighing and moaning on ilka green loaning -
The Flowers of the Forest are a' wede away.

In 1640, the Earl of Argyle took advantage of the absence of Lord Ogilvie, a staunch Jacobite who was away serving his King, to sack 'The Bonnie House o' Airlie'. It is now known as Forter Castle and remained a scorched ruin until restored in 1992. The poem tells of the brutal treatment of the high-spirited Lady Ogilvie, who refused to surrender to the hated enemy of her Clan.

Fordercastle.

THE BONNIE HOUSE o' AIRLIE   Anonymous

It fell on a day, a bonnie simmer day,
When green grew aits and barley,
That there fell out a great dispute
Between Argyle and Airlie.

Argyle has raised a hunder men,
An hunder harness'd rarely,
And he's awa' by the back of Dunkell,
To plunder the castle of Airlie.

Lady Ogilvie looks o'er her bower-window,
And O but she looks warely!
And there she spied the great Argyle,
Come to plunder the bonnie house of Airlie.

'Come down, come down, my Lady Ogilvie,
Come down and kiss me fairly.'
'O I winna kiss the fause Argyle,
If he shouldna leave a standing stane in Airlie.'

He hath taken her by the left shoulder,
Says, 'Dame, where lies thy dowry?'
'O it's east and west yon wan water side,
And it's down by the banks of the Airlie.'

They hae sought it up, they hae sought it down,
They hae sought it maist severely,
Till they fand it in the fair plum-tree
That shines on the bowling-green of Airlie.

He hath taken her by the middle sae small,
And O but she grat sairly!
And laid her down by the bonnie burn-side,
Till they plundered the castle of Airlie.

'Gif my gude lord war here this night,
As he is with King Charlie,
Neither you, nor ony ither Scottish lord,
Durst avow to the plundering of Airlie.

'Gif my gude lord war now at hame,
As he is with his king,
There durst nae a Campbell in a' Argyle
Set fit on Airlie green.

'Ten bonnie sons I have borne unto him,
The eleventh ne'er saw his daddy;
But though I had an hunder mair,
I'd gie them a' to King Charlie!'

This is another sad little poem lamenting the loss of loved ones in battle, and ending with a bitter attack on the savage Duke of Cumberland. I feel a bond with the lovely lass o' Inverness for, after the battle, Cumberland hanged my great-great-great-great-grandfather on a tree on Drumossie Moor:

LAMENT FOR CULLODEN   Robert Burns, 1759–1796

The lovely lass o' Inverness,
Nae joy nor pleasure can she see;
For e'en and morn she cries, 'Alas!'
And aye the saut tear blin's her e'e.

'Drumossie moor, Drumossie day,
A waefu' day it was to me!
For there I lost my father dear,
My father dear and brethren three.

Their winding-sheet the bluidy clay,
Their graves are growing green to see;
And by them lies the dearest lad
That ever blest a woman's e'e!

Now wae to thee, thou cruel lord,
A bluidy man I trow thou be;
For mony a heart thou hast made sair,
That ne'er did wrong to thine or thee.'

So much of Scottish poetry laments death and separation that I include just one that represents the other side of the coin – contentment, happiness, love in old age and certainty of a welcome in the World to Come:

THE LAND o' THE LEAL   Carolina, Lady Nairn, 1766–1845

I'm wearin' awa', John,
Like snaw-wreaths in thaw, John,
I'm wearin' awa'
To the land o' the leal.

There's nae sorrow there, John,
There's neither cauld nor care, John,
The day is aye fair
In the land o' the leal.

Our bonnie bairn's there, John.
She was baith gude and fair, John;
And O! we grudged her sair
To the land o' the leal.

But sorrow's sel' wears past, John,
And joy's a-coming fast, John,
The joy that's aye to last
In the land o' the leal.

Sae dear's the joy was bought, John,
Sae free the battle fought, John,
That sinfu' man e'er brought
To the land o' the leal.

O, dry your glistening e'e, John!
My saul langs to be free, John,
And angels beckon me
To the land o' the leal.

O, haud ye leal and true, John!
Your day it's wearin' through, John,
And I'll welcome you
To the land o' the leal.

Now fare-ye-weel, my ain John,
This world's cares are vain, John,
We'll meet, and we'll be fain,
In the land o' the leal.

We know that the Ettrick Shepherd visited Glenshee in about the year 1800, and I have often wondered if he found there the inspiration for this strange and beautiful poem. It is about a Scottish girl who fell asleep in a woodland glade. She was so chaste and pure that she was carried away by lovely beings to the Land of Thought, and I am sure that, if this happened anywhere, it must have been in the Glen of the Fairies.

KILMENY   James Hogg, 1770–1835 (extracts from a longer poem)

Bonnie Kilmeny gaed up the glen;
But it wasna to meet Duneira's men,
Nor the rosy monk of the isle to see,
For Kilmeny was pure as pure could be.
It was only to hear the yorlin sing,
And pu' the cress-flowers round the spring;
The scarlet hypp and the hindberrye,
And the nut that hung frae the hazel tree;
For Kilmeny was pure as pure could be.
But lang may her minny look o'er the wa',
And lang may she seek i' the green-wood shaw;
Lang the laird o' Duneira blame,
And lang, lang greet or Kilmeny come hame.

When many a day had come and fled,
When grief grew calm, and hope was dead,
When mass for Kilmeny's soul had been sung,

When the bedesman had pray'd and the dead bell rung,
Late, late in the gloamin' when all was still,
When the fringe was red on the westlin hill,
The wood was sere, the moon i' the wane,
The reek o' the cot hung over the plain,
Like a little wee cloud in the world its lane;
When the ingle low'd wi' an eiry leme,
Late, late in the gloamin' Kilmeny came hame.

'Kilmeny, Kilmeny, where have you been?
Lang hae we sought baith holt and den;
By linn, by ford, and green-wood tree,
Yet you are halesome and fair to see.
Where gat you that joup o' the lily scheen?
That bonnie snood of the birk sae green?
And these roses, the fairest that ever were seen?
Kilmeny, Kilmeny, where have you been?'

Kilmeny look'd up with a lovely grace,
But nae smile was seen on Kilmeny's face;
As still was her look, and as still was her e'e,
As the stillness that lay on the emerant lea,
Or the mist that sleeps on a waveless sea.
For Kilmeny had been she knew not where,
And Kilmeny had seen what she could not declare;

Kilmeny had been where the cock never crew,
Where the rain never fell, and the wind never blew,
But it seem'd as the harp of the sky had rung,
And the airs of heaven play'd round her tongue,

When she spake of the lovely forms she had seen,
And a land where sin had never been;
A land of love and a land of light,
Withouten sun, or moon, or night;
Where the rivers swa'd a living stream,
And the light a pure celestial beam;
The land of vision, it would seem,
A still, an everlasting dream.

In yon green-wood there is a waik,
And in that waik there is a wene.

In that green wene Kilmeny lay,
Her bosom happ'd wi' flowers gay;
But the air was soft and the silence deep,
And bonnie Kilmeny fell sound asleep.
She kenn'd nae mair, nor open'd her e'e,
Till waked by the hymns of a far countrye.
She 'waken'd on a couch of the silk sae slim,
All striped wi' the bars of the rinbow's rim;
And lovely beings round were rife,
Who erst had travell'd mortal life;
And aye they smiled and 'gan to speer,
'What spirit has brought this mortal here?'

'O bonnie Kilmeny! free frae stain,
If ever you seek the world again,
That world of sin, of sorrow and fear,
O tell of the joys that are waiting here;
And tell of the signs you shall shortly see;
Of the times that are now, and the times that shall be.'
They lifted Kilmeny, they led her away,
And she walk'd in the light of a sunless day;
The sky was a dome of crystal bright,
The fountain of vision, and fountain of light:

The emerald fields were of dazzling glow,
And the flowers of everlasting blow.
Then deep in the stream her body they laid,
That her youth and beauty never might fade;
And they smiled on heaven, when they saw her lie
In the stream of life that wander'd bye.

They bore her far to a mountain green,
To see what mortal never had seen;
And they seated her high on a purple sward,
And bade her heed what she saw and heard,
And note the changes the spirits wrought,
For now she lived in the land of thought.
She look'd, and she saw nor sun nor skies,
But a crystal dome of a thousand dyes:

She look'd, and she saw nae land aright,

But an endless whirl of glory and light:
And radiant beings went and came,
Far swifter than wind, or the linked flamme.
She hid her e'en frae the dazzling view;
She looked again and the scene was new.

But to sing the sights Kilmeny saw,
So far surpassing nature's law,
The singer's voice wad sink away,
And the string of his harp wad cease to play.
But she saw till the sorrows of man were bye,
And all was love and harmony;
Till the stars of heaven fell calmly away,
Like flakes of snaw on a winter day.

Then Kilmeny begged again to see
The friends she had left in her own countrye;
To tell of the place where she had been,
And the glories that lay in the land unseen;
To warn the living maidens fair,
The loved of Heaven, the spirits' care,
That all whose minds unmeled remain
Shall bloom in beauty when time is gane.

With distant music, soft and deep,
They lull'd Kilmeny sound asleep;
And when she waken'd she lay her lane,
All happed with flowers, in the green-wood wene.
When seven long years had come and fled,
When grief was calm, and hope was dead;
When scarce was remembered Kilmeny's name,
Late, late in a gloamin' Kilmeny came hame!
And O, her beauty was fair to see,
But still and steadfast was her e'e!
Such beauty bard may never declare,
For there was no pride nor passion there;
And the soft desire of a maiden's e'en
In that mild face could never be seen.

But wherever her peaceful form appear'd
The wild beasts of the hill were cheer'd;

The wolf play'd blythly round the field,
The lordly byson low'd and kneeled;
The dun deer woo'd with manner bland,
And cower'd aneath her lily hand.
And when at even the woodlands rung,
When hymns of other worlds she sung
In ecstasy of sweet devotion,
O, then the glen was all in motion!
The wild beasts of the forest came,
Broke from their bughts and faulds the tame,
And goved around, charm'd and amazed;
Even the dull cattle croon'd and gazed,
And murmur'd and look'd with anxious pain
For something the mystery to explain.

The buzzard came with the throstle-cock;
The corby left her houf in the rock;
The blackbird alang wi' the eagle flew;
The hind came tripping o'er the dew;
The hawk and the hern attour them hung,
And the merle and the mavis forhooy'd their young;
And all in a peaceful ring were hurl'd;
It was like an eve in a sinless world!

When a month and a day had come and gane,
Kilmeny sought the green-wood wene:
There laid her down on the leaves sae green,
And Kilmeny on earth was never mair seen.
But O, the words that fell from her mouth
Were words of wonder, and words of truth!
But all the land were in fear and dread,
For they kendna whether she was living or dead.
It wasna her hame, she couldna remain;
She left this world of sorrow and pain,
And returned to the land of thought again.

The following are all poems about Glenshee. I have found most of them in books given to my uncle – books by the Reverend T.D.Miller, Lady Ashmore, John Grant and others. Some are from old newspapers and family records.

The first is one which was taught to the young people of the Glen in the last century. We do not know the author but, from the strength of his sentiments and his knowledge of the battle, it is probable that he was a local man. The only way his account differs from all the others I have heard and read is that he describes the valiant miller as a Glenisla man. Might it just be possible that the author was a Glenisla man himself?

THE BATTLE OF THE CAIRNWALL (CAIRNWELL)

The mountain gale unheeded twists
The golden locks of Allac Bane
As breathless still she stands and lists
And thinks she hears the words again.

The faltering sigh-borne word, 'Farewell'
That closed her Allan's latest kiss;
How sweet on fancy's ear it fell
As if 'twere breathed on hymns of bliss.

For Allac felt, she knew not how,
The sun rose on her bridal morn,
And long before he kissed the dew,
Her Allan from her side was torn.

For down the rocks, where Isla rolled,
A roving band of cat'rans poured;
And hill and dale, and byre and fold,
Before the opening dawn were scoured.

The cross-tar flew, the signals wave,
The cat'rans on the Cairnwall brow;
Glenshee, the generous and the brave,
Arose to check the common foe.

The brave Cam-Ruadh led the train,
The archer-chief, and by his side
Young Allan bounded up the Glen
And left behind his bonnie bride.

Behind the mountain's rocky brow,
The ruffians lurked among the heath,
And he who dared to pass below
Rushed on the barbed points of death.

Cam-Ruadh, cautious, marked their state,
While Isla's sons arose in sight,
'Here for our comrades let us wait
And in a body join the fight.'

'Let cowards wait, come on Glenshee,'
The brave but reckless Allan cried,
'Who follows not, a coward he.'
'We follow all,' Glenshee replied.

Wild flashed Cam-Ruadh's single eye,
Proud throbbed his heart on passion's thorn,
'Then go,' he said, 'Like bullocks die,
Glenisla's dupes, the cat'rans' scorn!'

'But if I by the morning's rays,
As friend or foe, an arrow aim,
A coward let me close my days,
A coward as ye give the name.'

Then down between two sheltering stones
He sat. Young Allan sought his foes;
And cheering cries and wailing groans
Soon from the unequal combat rose.

Glenisla, from the height adown
Beheld the fierce unequal fray;
They knew the quarrel was their own,
But saw and felt their own the prey.

But fie! forget the part they bore,
Blot out the deed in pity's tear:
But they had one, the Miller Mhor,
Remember him, his name is dear.

Shamed at his friends, he sought his foes,
Strong was his arm, and great his might,
And frequent fell his fatal blows,
And many felt their deadly weight.

Deep drank his dirk of cat'ran blood,
As daring wild, he scoured the bole,
Till sixteen arrows sapped the flood
That kept afloat his gallant soul.

161

Keen fought Glenshee, scarce one to four
Of what the hardy cat'rans were;
But well they plied their little power
And showed what native courage dare.

With nervous arm they bent the bow,
And many a foeman nipp'd the heath,
And many a Sheeman pointed low,
And fast went on the work of death.

But oh! Cam-Ruadh's vow was pain,
To many a friend his heart was sore,
And oft he cursed the Isla men
And oft the impassioned oath he swore!

At length the lingering shadows turned,
The fatal oath-bound hour went by.
He rose! revenge his bosom burned,
'Revenge,' he cried, 'my friends, or die.'

'And hear my simple counsel now,
And only half-string bend the bow;
Your arrows glide too strongly through,
They pierce, but cannot hurt the foe.'

Their shouts re-echoed through the hill,
They hailed Cam-Ruadh to the strife,
And plied their shafts with deadly skill
Into the cat'rans' springs of life.

The captain of the lawless band
Beheld Cam-Ruadh's red locks wave,
Full well he knew his fatal hand,
His shafts a summons to the grave.

'The bounding deer's my arrow's aim,
'Twill catch the eagle soaring high:
But make me not Cam-Ruadh's aim,
And safe my shafts shall pass him by.'

'Point at my heart, my bosom's bare.'
The indignant, brave Cam-Ruadh cried;
'Spare not, for I shall never spare.'
The arrow flew – the ruffian died.

Death danced exulting on the string
And drove the unerring shafts before,
Till fifty dipped their eagle wing
Into the cat'rans' vital gore.

The remnant fled, the gory vale
Now stained, the trembling widows' tread,
And lovers mourn the daring dead,
And mothers join the cronach wail.

The mountain gale, unheeded, twists
The golden locks of Allac Bane,
As Allan's cold, pale lips she kissed,
Those lips she ne'er would kiss again.

'On the 6th September, 1715,' says the *Deeside Guide*, 'John Erskine, the 39th Earl of Mar, having marched from Glenlivat, where he had proclaimed the Chevalier de St George under the title of James VIII, erected his standard at Castletown of Braemar, amidst a great assemblage of his vassals. The standard was made by the Countess of Mar and was of a gorgeous bright blue colour, having on one side the arms of Scotland, richly embroidered in gold; and on the other the brave thistle of Scotland, with these words underneath, 'No Union', and on the top the ancient motto, 'Nemo me impune lacessit.' You may judge if there was not shouting and blowing of trumpets when this brave standard was upreared, and its rich silken folds unfurled to the free winds. But even in that hour of triumph there happened an occurrence which threw a visible gloom over the spirits of

the superstitious Highlanders; this was that the gilt ball which ornamented the top fell down to the ground, as they thought, an omen of evil bode to the cause they were that day engaging in. I should mention that the standard had two pendants of white ribbon, on one of which was written 'For our King and oppressed country'; and on the other 'For our lives and liberties'.

The standard was raised on a little mound or knoll a few yards east of what is now the Invercauld Arms, on the south side of the road, and it was noted, 'How welcome were the broadswords of the Broughdeargs ... and all the swords of Glenshee and Glenisla gleaming round the chiefs'.

This little ditty was sung as the brave Highlanders marched over the Cairnwell and down through Glenshee:

> The standard on the Braes of Mar
> Is up and streaming rarely;
> The gathering-pipe on Lochnagar
> Is sounding lang and sairly.
> The Highland men
> Frae hill and glen,
> In martial hue,
> Wi' bonnets blue,
> Wi' belted plaids,
> An' burnished blades,
> Are coming late and early.
>
> Wha wadna join our noble chief,
> The Drummond and Glengary,
> Macgregor, Murray, Rollo, Keith,
> Panmure and gallant Harry?
> Macdonald's men,
> Clan-Ranald's men,
> Mackenzie's men,
> Macgillivray's men,
> Strathallan's men,
> The Lowlan' men
> Of Callender and Airly.
>
> Fy! Donald, up, an' let's awa,
> We canna longer parley,
> When Jamie's back is at the wa',
> The lad we lo'e sae dearly,

We'll go – we'll go,
An' seek the foe
An' fling the plaid,
An' swing the blade,
An' forward dash,
An' hack and slash,
An' fleg the German carlie.

The remaining poems are less warlike and tell of either homely domestic incidents or the nostalgia of those who have left the Glen.

One of the best known consisted originally of seven verses, but unfortunately only two verses now survive. It tells how a Perth man found the lass of his dreams in Glenshee and how eventually, after much persuasion and maidenly hesitation, she consented to become his bride and make her home in the Fair City.

LASS O' GLENSHEE

When honey-dip'd bells on the heather were spreading,
An' Hieland hills hum'd wi' the far-travell'd bee,
I found a fair maiden, as hame I was ridin',
A-hirding her sheep on the Hill o' Glenshee.

The rose on her cheek saftly press'd by a dimple,
Blushed red wi' the light o' her lovely bit e'e;
She looked sae inchantin', sae sweet and sae simple,
My heart soon belonged to the lass o' Glenshee.

Weel Bertha may boast o' her lasses sae bonny,
Since Scotland for beauties has gi'en her the grace,
But search ilka corner I doubt if she's ony
Could stand near the lassie I brought frae Glenshee;

To match wi' my Jenny, O wha is't would venture,
She's sweet as the zephyr that plays round the pea,
She's spotless and pure as the robes o' the winter
When spread out to bleach on the hills o' Glenshee.

The author of this poem was Andrew Sharpe, a cobbler from Bridgend, Perth, so it may well tell the story of his own love. He was a man of many talents – a poet, musician and painter as well as a cobbler; but, sadly, he died in 1817 at the young age of thirty five. He is buried in Kinnoull Churchyard where his tombstone can still be seen inscribed with his own words:

'Halt for a moment, passenger, and read,
Here Andrew doses in his last bed,
Silent his flute and torn off the key,
His pencils scattered, and the Muse set free.'

The next song was composed by William Thomson who was the postmaster in Kennoway, Fife, in the early years of the last century. It describes not only a lover's feelings, but also gives a vivid picture of the changing seasons in the Glen:

THE SHEPHERD OF GLENSHEE

I wander over hill and dale;
I breathe the healthful mountain gale:
Far from the city's busy throng,
I listen to the warbler's song.
I guide and tend my fleecy flocks
Amongst the muirs, around the rocks,
And wander unconfined and free,
By bank and burn amid Glenshee.

(Dog) Violet

While roaming o'er the mountain side,
I mark the season's onward glide;
See winter clothe the hills with snow,
And make the rivers overflow;
Behold the sunshine and the showers
In spring renew the leafless bowers;
And list the hum of busy bee,
Among the blossoms in Glenshee.

When summer shines on howm and height,
And fills the bosom with delight;
When bloom adorns the sylvan dell,
And purple heath flowers deck the fell;
At gloaming grey amid the glade,
I wander with my mountain maid;
And there is none like her I see,
The fairest flower in all Glenshee!

I love to mark, begemmed with dew,
In shady dell, the violet blue;
I joy to view the crystal stream
In morning's cloudless radiance gleam;
But dearer, sweeter, lovelier far
Than opening rose or shining star –
Than all I know, than all I see,
The blossom that adorns Glenshee!

The following plea by the old stone bridge at the Spital was made in the 1920s. It was almost uncanny in its foresight, but it was another sixty years before a new bridge was built to relieve the strain on its old 'humpit back'. It remains one of the most beautiful landmarks in the Glen and a fine tribute to the skill of Britain's greatest roadbuilder.

THE AULD BRIG'S PLEA

Oh! I hae viewed the swollen flood,
And hear't the Boreal blast;
And I hae stayed the summer trade
A hunner years by-past.
The lumb'rin' coach, the creakin' wain,
Hae crossed my humpit back,
And mony royal retinues
Gaed princin' ower the track.

The Wade Bridge, S. of Glenshee. 4/2000

But noo the cars an' charabancs
Come birlin' up the road,
And I am growin' old an frail,
An' canna' thole their load.
For motor tractor's awfu' draught
Wade never thocht to plan;
Nor dreamt to guage for mod'rn craft,
Like lang-spanned charabang.

My back is scarr'd wi' mony a tare,
Forby the strain and stress,
The burdens that I'm ca'ed to bear,
Words canna' weel express.
Folk say I'm antiquated noo,
For fashions change wi' time;
And metal girders, laid in raws,
Tak' place o' stane an' lime.

It's no for me to br'ak my he'rt,
Or raise an unco stoor;
They'll need a brig o' braider mak',
Wi' less o' curvature;
Sae, when they rule to tak' me doon,
And set the lattice trig,
I'm fain ye'll hae a kindly thocht
For Wade an' his Auld Brig!

The next four poems are from a little volume called *Songs of Glenshee* by Lady
Ashmore. The first tells of an incident which took place on the road through
the Glen and demonstrates very clearly why our Kings and Queens have been
so much loved by their subjects. Those gracious waves will certainly have been
remembered for a lifetime:

THE ROYAL ROAD

'The King and Queen are passing today' –
The word, like wildfire, went all through the land –
And gathered in groups by the King's Highway,
Are his loyal subjects on either hand.

Far up in Glenshee, in a lonely spot,
Where silence is broken by mountain rills,
Stands an old grey cottage, with garden-plot,
Half hidden in a fold of the purple hills.

There a lame child waits, full of trembling hope –
She has heard by chance that the Motor Car
May pass by her home, on the heather slope,
When the King and Queen go back to Braemar.

She has heard of flags – and no flag has she –
But Oh! she can cheer as well as them all,
And throw a white rose from Prince Charlie's tree,
Where the King and Queen can see it fall.

When the longed-for moment at last has come,
The Royal Car passed and she tried to stand –
But alas! excitement had made her dumb,
And the rose was still in her small, hot hand.

She forgot to throw and forgot to cheer,
Yet the happiest heart in all Glenshee
Is the heart of the child who boasts, ''Twas here
The King and the Queen waved their hands to me.'

EXILED

Over here are mighty mountains,
Waving woods and fairy fountains;
But to me,
There is nothing like the heather
And the hills we roamed together
In Glenshee.

All around are flowers in splendour,
But no blossoms bring such tender
Thoughts to me,
As the bluebells and the gowans
And the red, red of the rowans
In Glenshee.

Here are many waters gushing,
But no roaring river rushing
Calls to me
Like the one, when shades are falling,
That across the sea is calling
From Glenshee.

'Oh, come home!' I hear it saying,
While I keep on hoping, praying
That might be –
For such memories are waking
That my heart is almost breaking
For Glenshee!

My last poem has nothing to do with Glenshee and I include it for no reason at all, which is probably as good a reason as any. It is about a naughty (if you are a good Catholic you may say a *very* naughty) girl from Edinburgh, quite unlike the pure and chaste Kilmeny; but let us not condemn her for she seems to have found true happiness at last, and anyway, be honest, which of the two would you rather have as a companion at a ceilidh?

KISS'D YESTREEN

Kiss'd yestreen, and kiss'd yestreen,
Up the Gallowgate, down the Green;
I've woo'd wi' lords, and woo'd wi' lairds.
I've mooled wi' carles and melled wi' cairds,
I've kissed wi' priests – 'twas done i' the dark,
Twice in my gown and thrice in my sark;
But priest, nor lord, nor loon can gie
Sic kindly kisses as he gae me.

18 *Hospitality and some Highland Dishes*

Often, often, often
Goes the Christ in the stranger's guise.

So says the ancient Gaelic proverb, and indeed there were few places in the world where the traveller could find hospitality and good manners to equal those of the Highlander and his family.

Even in the poorest cottage this was so, and we have from Alexander Carmichael a truly delightful description of the welcome he received in a Highland croft 150 years ago:

The house was clean and comfortable, if plain and unpretending, most things in it being home-made. There were three girls in the house, young, comely and shy, and four women, middle-aged, handsome and picturesque in their homespun gowns and high-crowned mutches. Three of the women had been to the moorland pastures with their cattle, and had turned in here to rest on their way home.

'Hail to the house and household,' said I, greeting the inmates in the salutation of our fathers.

'Hail to you, kindly stranger,' replied the housewife. 'Come forward and take this seat. If it be not ill-mannered, may we ask whence you have come today? ... May the Possessor keep you in his own keeping, good man! You have left early and travelled far, and must be hungry.'

With this the woman raised her eyes towards her daughters, standing demurely silent and motionless as Greek statues in the background. In a moment the three fair girls became active and animated. One ran to the stack and brought in an armful of hard black peats, another ran to the well and brought in a pail full of clear spring water, while the third quickly spread a cloth, white as snow, upon the table in the inner room. The three neighbour women rose to leave, and I rose to do the same.

'Where are you going, good man?' asked the housewife in injured surprise, moving between me and the door. 'You must not go till you eat a bit and drink a sip. That indeed would be a reproach to us that we would not soon get over ... Food will be ready presently, and in the meantime you will bathe your feet and dry your stockings which are wet after coming through the marshes of the moorland.'

Then the woman went down on her knees and washed and dried the feet of the stranger as tenderly as a mother would those of her child.

In an incredibly short time I was asked to go 'ben' and break bread. The table was laden with wholesome food, sufficient for several persons. There were fried herrings and boiled turbot, fresh from the sea, and eggs fresh from the yard. There were fresh butter and salt butter, wheaten scones, barley bannocks and oatcakes, with excellent tea and cream. The woman apologised that she had no 'aran coinnich' (moss bread, that is, loaf bread) and no biscuits, they being simple crofter folk away from the big town.

In the laird's house too, there was always a cheerful welcome, and Dr Johnson in 1786 wrote of his visit to the Isle of Raasay. 'We were introduced to the house, which one of the company called 'the Court of Rasay' with politeness which not the Court of Versailles could have thought defective.'

Boswell describes the evening:

It was past six o'clock when we arrived. Some excellent brandy was served round immediately, according to the custom of the Highlands, where a dram is generally taken every day. They call it a 'scalch'. On a sideboard was placed for us, who had come off the sea, a substantial dinner and variety of wines. Then we had coffee and tea. I observed in the room several elegantly bound books and other marks of improved life. Soon afterwards a fiddler appeared and a little ball began. Rasay himself danced with as much spirit as any man, and Malcolm bounded like a roe. Sandie MacLeod, who has at times an excessive flow of spirits ... made much jovial noise. Dr Johnson was so delighted with this scene that he said, 'I know not how we shall get away.' We had a company of thirty at supper, and all was good humour and gaiety, without intemperance.

The learned Doctor, undoubtedly the greatest talker of his (or any) age, though not uniformly pleased with all he found in Scotland, would, I am sure, have approved as much of the old saying '*Cha'n fhiach cuirm gun a comluadh*' (A feast is nothing without its conversation) as he did of the breakfast he ate the next morning:

> In the breakfast the Scots, whether of the Lowlands or of the mountains, must be confessed to excel us … If an epicure could remove by a wish in quest of sensual gratification, wherever he had supped, he would breakfast in Scotland.

Two hundred years later the tradition of hospitality was as strong as ever and no visitor to Finegand was allowed to depart without joining the household for a meal, and I well remember that when the big sheep lorries arrived early on the morning of a sale day, they were never loaded until the drivers had been into the house for their breakfast.

That is how we lived in the Glen and I pray that it will never change.

In the words of Robbie Burns:

> When death's dark stream I'll ferry o'er,
> A time that surely will come –
> In Heaven itself I'll ask no more
> Than just a Highland welcome.

Though generous in the extreme in his hospitality, the Highlander was by nature abstemious in both food and drink. I have already quoted Donald Ramsay, whose motto was 'Drink little that you may drink long', and there are many other Scots proverbs in the same vein:

> 'Licht suppers mak' lang life.'
> 'Surfits slay mair than swords.'
> 'He that eats but ae dish seldom needs the doctor.'

With the exception of tea, coffee and French wines in the laird's house, everything in the kitchen was produced at home; but simple though the fare may have been, it was always prepared with the utmost care and delicacy.

The traditional Highland dishes described here are those which I have known and enjoyed all my life, and Lady Claire Macdonald has graciously agreed to describe their preparation and cooking.

BRAISED VENISON WITH VEGETABLES AND MILK

A haunch of venison, about 10lb, (4.5kg)

4 tablespoons sunflower seed oil

4 oz (125g) butter

2 large onions, peeled and chopped

4 carrots, peeled and chopped

2 parsnips, peeled and chopped

4 leeks, washed and sliced

2 cloves of garlic, peeled and finely chopped

salt and freshly ground black pepper

1 pint (600ml) milk

2 oz (50g) plain flour

½ pint (300ml) red wine

1 rounded tablespoon redcurrant jelly

For the marinade

1 pint (600ml) sunflower seed oil

2 onions, peeled and sliced

2 carrots peeled and sliced

2 cloves of garlic, peeled and chopped

1 pint (600ml) red wine

½ pint (300ml) red wine vinegar

6 juniper berries, crushed with the end of a rolling pin

a bouquet garni

To make the marinade, heat the oil and brown the vegetables and garlic. Remove from the heat and stir in all the other ingredients. Leave to go quite cold, then pour over the venison, which should be in a deep dish. Cover and leave it - marinating in a cool place for 2 days; baste the meat twice a day with the marinade.

When you are ready to cook, take the venison out of the marinade and pat it dry with kitchen paper. Heat the oil and 2oz (50g) butter in a roasting tin, and brown the venison well all over. Lift the haunch out of the roasting tin and put all the prepared vegetables and the garlic into the tin. Season with salt and freshly ground black pepper, and put the meat on top of the vegetables. Put into a hot oven, 425°F, 220°C, gas mark 7, for 30 minutes.

Remove the tin from the oven and pour the milk over the meat. Cover the tin with a double thickness of foil, wrapping it down round the edge of the tin tightly. Put in a low oven, 300°F, 150°C, gas mark 2, for 3 hours.

Remove from the oven, and put the venison on a dish to keep warm. Let the vegetables and the juices in the tin cool, then puree them in a blender. In a large saucepan melt the remaining butter. Stir in the flour and cook for 2 minutes. Stir the red wine into the flour and butter, bring to the boil, then stir in the pureed vegetables and the redcurrant jelly. Check the seasoning, adding a little more salt and pepper if you think it needs it. Carve the venison and serve the sauce either poured over the slices, or handed round separately in a sauce boat.

GAME SOUP

An essential ingredient of game soup is a good game stock, so this is a two-stage recipe – first the stock, then the soup. It is an ideal way to use old grouse. Carcasses from cooked birds can be used to make the stock, but it is not quite as good as when made from uncooked bones.

Serves 8

For the stock

> 2–3 game carcasses, preferably from uncooked birds such as pigeon, grouse or pheasant
> 4 pints (2.5 litres) water
> 3 onions, peeled and each stuck with a few cloves
> 2 celery sticks
> small handful of black peppercorns
> 1 tsp rock salt (kosher salt)
> 1 bouquet garni

For the soup

> 2 oz/4 tbsp (60g) butter
> 2 bacon rashers (slices) chopped
> 2 onions, peeled and chopped
> 2 carrots, peeled and chopped
> 2 potatoes, peeled and chopped
> 1 large garlic clove, peeled and chopped

pared rind of ½ lemon and ½ orange

3–4 juniper berries, bashed with the end of a rolling pin

1 tbsp redcurrant jelly

salt and freshly ground black pepper

½ pint (300ml) port wine.

Put all the stock ingredients into a large saucepan and cover with a lid. If you are using uncooked carcasses, bring the water to simmering point, then drain off and measure 4 pints (2.5 litres) of fresh water into the pan and bring to a simmering point once more (remember to add another tsp of salt). Once the water has reached a gentle simmer, cook, covered, for 3 hours. Cool, and strain the stock. Keep in the refrigerator and freeze the surplus stock for making game soup another time.

Melt the butter in a large saucepan and add the bacon and onions; cook over moderate heat until the onions are soft and translucent, then add the carrots, potatoes, garlic, lemon and orange rind and juniper berries. Cook for a further few minutes, then pour in 2 pints (1.25 litres) of game stock. Half cover the pan with lid and simmer gently for 40–45 minutes. Cool a bit, then liquidise, adding the redcurrant jelly to the soup in the liquidiser. Sieve the liquidised soup – game soup should be velvety smooth – and season to taste with salt and pepper. Add the port, and reheat to serve, garnished, if you like, with small croutons mixed with chopped parsley.

This soup freezes very well.

ROWAN AND APPLE JELLY

Rowan jelly can be awfully bitter, which is why I put apples in mine. I also like to add a cinnamon stick, to give a subtle and barely discernable hint of spice to the jelly.

Makes about 6 lbs (2.8 kg)

2 lbs (900g) rowan berries

2 lbs (900g) eating apples – any sort except Golden Delicious, which are tasteless – quartered

4 pints (2.5 litres) water

1 cinnamon stick

2 lbs (900g) sugar

Into a large saucepan, put the rowan berries, quartered apples, water and cinnamon stick. Bring the water to a simmer and cook, with the pan half covered, for 35-40 minutes or until the berries can be squashed against the sides of the pan with the back of your wooden spoon and the pieces of apple are soft. Strain the liquid from the cooked fruit through a jelly bag (or muslin or teacloth) into a bowl. Don't be tempted to squeeze the contents of the jelly bag; just let it drip for several hours, until all the liquid has dripped through.

Put the liquid from the bowl into a clean saucepan and add the sugar. Over a moderate heat stir to dissolve the sugar completely, then let the liquid boil fast for 10-15 minutes before testing for a set: remove the pan from the heat, drip some of the jelly onto a saucer and leave for a few minutes to cool, then push the surface with your finger. If it fails to wrinkle, boil up the liquid for a further five minutes before testing for a set once more.

Pot into warmed jars and seal. Label the jars and store in a cool place.

OVEN SCONES

We make scones like these every day at Kinloch Lodge – for ourselves and the guests. They are much nicer made and eaten straight away.

> Makes 20–24
>
> 1½ lb (700g) self-raising flour
> 1 tsp salt
> 2 rounded tsp baking powder
> 2 tbs golden (light corn) syrup
> 2 size 1 eggs, beaten
> 2 tbs sunflower oil
> about ¾ pint (450ml) milk
> (to make 1 pint (600ml) when combined with the eggs)

Sift the flour, salt and baking powder into a large mixing bowl. Mix together the syrup, beaten eggs, sunflower oil and milk, and gradually add this to the dry ingredients.

Flour a tabletop or work surface, and tip the dough onto it. With floured hands, pat the dough smooth, patting it out to a thickness of about 1 inch (2.5cm) – the dough is too damp to roll out with a rolling pin satisfactorily. Cut into circles with a scone cutter and put the scones on a baking sheet.

Bake in a preheated hot oven 425°F, 220°C, gas mark 7, for 12–15 minutes. Serve warm.

OATCAKES

Makes about 35–40

8 oz (225g) self raising flour
1 tsp bicarbonate of soda (baking soda)
1 tsp salt
1 lb (450g) pinhead oatmeal (coarse Scotch oats)
5 oz (150g) butter or margerine
3 fl oz (90ml) each water and milk mixed together

Sift the flour, soda and salt into a bowl and stir in oatmeal. Rub the butter or margerine into the dry ingredients, then stir in the milk and water mixture. Sift some extra flour onto a table or work surface and roll out the dough. Cut into rounds about 2 inches (5cm) in diameter, and carefully lift them onto a baking sheet.

Bake in a preheated moderate oven, 350°F, 180°C, gas mark 4, until pale golden brown, 10-12 minutes. Cool on a wire rack. When the oatcakes are quite cold, store them in an airtight container.

To freshen up oatcakes which have been kept for several days, heat them on a baking sheet in a moderate oven for 5 minutes – they taste slightly toasted and are delicious.

SCOTTISH PANCAKES

Makes 20–24

1¼ teacups plain flour
¼ cup sugar
½ rounded teaspoon bicarbonate of soda
1 rounded teaspoon cream of tartar
pinch of salt
1 egg, beaten
½ large breakfast cup of milk
oil for cooking

Sieve the dry ingredients together, and stir in the egg and milk until the mixture is well blended. If possible, make up the batter in advance and leave it to sit for a few hours.

With my Aga, I lift the lid of the cooler hot plate about 20 minutes before I intend to make the pancakes, and oil the surface, then put spoonsful of the mixture onto the hot surface. When bubbles appear all over the surface of each pan-cake, they are ready to be turned over using a fish slice or large palette knife. If you don't have an Aga, use a griddle or large frying pan. They are best eaten still warm from the cooking.

Pancakes freeze well.

To add to these absolutely delicious recipes from Lady Macdonald, I would like to mention one or two rather more homely ones from my own family.

SCOTCH BROTH OR BARLEY BROTH

> 3 lbs neck of lamb
> barley
> peas
> carrots
> turnips
> onions
> parsley

Put the neck of lamb into a saucepan and add 6 pints of cold water, a quarter of a pound of Scots barley and a teaspoonful of salt. Add to this a large cupful of split grey peas. Let the broth boil slowly for an hour, skimming off any scum that may arise, and then add two young diced carrots and turnips and two or three sliced onions. Quarter of an hour before the broth is ready, add a little chopped parsley. Serve in a tureen and skim off any fat on the surface.

This wonderful broth is more, much more, than just a soup. It is a whole meal in itself, and it brings back two very clear and fond memories. The first is of my early school days, when it appeared on the table once a week, and the second is of my old friend Nicky Norman, Keeper of the Armoury at Edinburgh Castle and later at the Tower of London. Nicky was a great raconteur and among his fund of Scottish stories was one about Scotch Broth.

Apparently, one day the Prince Regent was crossing a Highland loch in a steamer and was drawn to the galley by the appetizing aroma of Scotch Broth. He approached the cook who did not recognise him.

'How is it made?' he asked.

'Weel, there's mutton intill't, there's neeps intill't, there's peas intill't . . .

'What is intill't?'

'I'm tellin' ye, mon, there's mutton intill't, there's neeps intill't, there's . . .

'Yes, yes, but what is *intill't?*'

'Gudesakes, mon, am I no' thrang tellin' ye what's intill't? There's mutton intill't, there's …'

This embarrassing impasse was only brought to an end by the timely arrival of one of the Prince's staff, who explained that 'intill't' simply meant 'in it' or 'into it'. I have heard that the Prince took Gaelic lessons from some of the ghillies at Balmoral, but clearly he never mastered broad Scots.

Lastly, a word or two about porridge, the most famous of all Scottish dishes.

> Oatmeal
> Salt
> Water – certainly best from a Highland spring.

For each person allow one breakfastcupful of water. Add a generous handful of Scottish oatmeal and a small saltspoonful of salt. Bring the water to the boil and add the oatmeal in a steady rain from the left hand while stirring briskly with a porridge stick or spirtle held in the right hand. For the best porridge – and to ensure good luck – always stir in a clockwise direction. Take care to avoid lumps. Add the salt after about ten minutes boiling. In 30 minutes the porridge should be ready, but an alternative method of cooking, always used by my mother, was to prepare the breakfast porridge in the evening. After 10 minutes boiling, the pot was transferred to a hay box or a cool oven, where it continued to cook slowly all night. When the hungry family came running downstairs in the morning, there was the porridge, ready and waiting.

Traditionally, it was always eaten standing with one's back to the fire, but we, as a family, always sat round the table. We ate it with thick fresh cream and occasionally, to the stern disapproval of my father, with a spoonful of brown sugar or honey.

With or without these accompaniments, there is no other way to start the day in Scotland.

19 Malt Whisky

Edradour

No book about Glenshee would be complete without some reference to *'uisge beatha'* or 'mountain dew' as my family called it.

The origins of this glorious spirit are shrouded in mystery, but are probably more recent than many Scots believe. Until the 17th century, beer was the drink of the ordinary Highlander and claret that of the laird and his family. You will remember that when the Cam Ruadh gave shelter to his former enemies in a storm 'a sheep was brought in from the fold to satisfy their hunger and was washed down by *a cogie of good ale'*.

Whisky was then a luxury, but its growing popularity was seen by Parliament as a welcome source of revenue (what's new?) and in 1644 a devastating tax of 2*s*. 8*d*. (13p) was imposed on a pint of 'strong liquor'. Many small tenant farmers for whom the sale of whisky had been a welcome – even a vital – addition to their income, were faced with real hardship. They ignored the tax and continued to distil illegally. Overnight, an entire cottage industry took to the hills, and Glenshee and the neighbouring glens were no exception.

The wild and remote corries of the Cairnwell and Glas Maol were ideal for such work, and very soon the authorities began to realise that imposing a malt tax was one thing, but collecting it was quite another matter.

Although the work of the illicit distiller was hard and risky, the potential reward made it well worth while (one contemporary estimate calculated that an outlay of £1 could bring a return of £7 from those who enjoyed the product but were unable or afraid to distil it themselves) and those involved in the trade soon learnt to conceal their operations from the 'king's men'.

The siting of the stills was of the utmost importance, and three things were necessary.

First, a supply of clear spring water, second a place where the tell-tale peat reek would not be too noticeable, and third, a clear view for the look-out who could give warning of approaching strangers.

Small, sturdy ponies carried the barley up into the hills by night where willing hands unloaded the sacks and laid them to soak in the stream-bed. After a period of time dictated by experience, the contents were spread out to germinate on the dry earth floors of carefully hidden stores or cellars. Then, after a few days came the toughest and most dangerous part of the operation. The 'green' sprouting barley had to be dried over smoking peat fires, and it was here that detection became most likely as the crofters, red-eyed and choking, malted the barley on a mesh of crossed sticks over a pit of glowing peat. But, dangerous and uncomfortable as this rich earthy smoke may have been, nevertheless it was, and still is, an essential ingredient in giving the finished whisky its distinctive flavour.

Next, the malted barley was taken away to a local mill where it was ground into 'grist'. Then came another night-time journey as the grist was carried to the secret still. Here it was tipped into barrels filled with soft and often slightly peaty water from the burn and the mixture was carefully stirred with sticks which ancient wisdom demanded should be cut only from birch or willow.

The still itself, or 'black pot' as it was affectionately known in the Highlands, was made of copper and equipped with a distinctive spiral worm to cool the evaporating spirit. It was a fairly conspicuous object in a Highland corrie and, when not in use, had to be dismantled and carefully hidden, often in some deep pool in the burn.

As the years passed, the illicit distillers became more sophisticated and efficient and a network of agents grew up all over Scotland, and even down into England where the unique and unrivalled qualities of mountain dew were just beginning to be appreciated.

Inevitably, of course, the excisemen had some successes, but seizing the whisky was not the end of their task. The casks still had to be delivered to the Board of Excise. This often meant a considerable journey and I once heard of such a gauger who was determined to take no chances with his valuable cargo. He took it upstairs with him to his bedroom in the local inn, but was bewildered and dismayed to find it empty in the morning. The former owners, no doubt with the connivance of the landlord, and armed with a well-aimed drill, had bored a hole through the floor and into the cask and recovered what they had worked so hard to produce.

By the early 1800s however, Parliament began to realise that the only way to curb the blackmarket was to make conditions more reasonable and attractive for legal distilling. Suitable legislation was passed in 1823 and the days of the illicit still were numbered.

Today, whisky is produced in four main regions of Scotland – Lowland, Highland, Speyside and the Islands, and each area has its own characteristics. There are literally hundreds of malt whiskies and I cannot claim to have tasted more than a generous handful of them, but I have my favourites from each of the last three regions and I give them to you with pleasure.

Highland – Edradour.

Speyside – The Macallan, Cragganmore.

Island – Lagavulin, Talisker.

HIGHLAND REGION

The jewel in the crown of this region is undoubtedly Edradour, Scotland's smallest and prettiest distillery, situated in a lovely little glen just a few miles from Finegand.

Here, little has changed in the last hundred and fifty years and the distillery is probably the only one left in Scotland where the whisky is still hand-made by the old well-tried traditional methods. These, combined with the soft, ice-cold water from Moulin Moor and specially grown local barley account for its unique character and flavour. It is one of only a handful of Highland malts which are still matured in oak sherry casks, and it is from these that it derives its beautiful pale honey colour.

It is a rich, creamy, after-dinner whisky with a rather spicy taste and a delightful subtle smokiness.

SPEYSIDE

The Macallan has often been called the Rolls Royce of single malts and few, I think, would disagree with that.

Tradition says that it has been created at a fording place on the River Spey since mediaeval times, and it was certainly one of the first on Speyside to be produced legally, under licence, in 1824.

What has made it supreme among its peers since then has been the relentless determination of the distillers to let nothing – absolutely nothing, and especially financial reward – interfere with the quality of the product. Only Golden Promise barley – a low-yielding and uneconomic variety, but superb for whisky making – is used and the stills are some of the smallest in Scotland. As at Edradour, every drop of the whisky is matured in oak sherry casks, and in spite of the

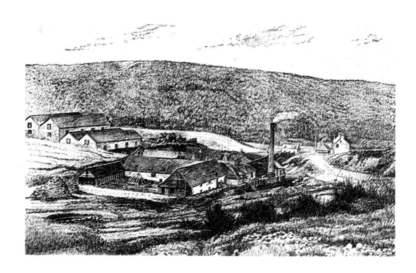

increasing difficulty of finding these, I am glad to say that the Macallan distillery seems to have a reliable source, for the influence of these casks is an essential part of the character of the Macallan.

To sum up this magnificent whisky, let me quote Alan Milner, the Dean of Trinity, my old College at Oxford, 'The Macallan which, to me sits at the peak of Speyside quality ... is mellow gold, its flavour slightly sweet, malty and smoky with a hint of peat.'

Though perhaps not as well-known as the Macallan, 12 year old Cragganmore is one of the most subtle, fragrant and delightful of all the malt whiskies produced in Scotland.

The charming little distillery, hidden in a hollow high above the Spey, was founded by John Smith in 1869 and has several characteristics which together create such a distinctive whisky.

First is the water, which comes from nearby springs and is relatively hard for the district. Next is the unusual design of the stills which are flat-topped with an L shaped head leading into the lye pipe. This results in reflux – a sort of double distillation – with only the lighter vapours passing through the lye pipe to create a wonderfully clean, complex malt. Finally, it is matured, unlike Edradour and the Macallan, almost entirely in old bourbon casks.

The end result is a lovely golden whisky, smooth, fragrant and delicate, with a long, gentle finish. Sip this malt in January (or any other time) and it will remind you of meadow grass, summer flowers and the herbs along the river bank.

THE ISLANDS

The Island malts are as different from those of the Highlands and Speyside as it is possible to imagine. If Cragganmore is a gentle breeze carrying the scent of summer flowers, Lagavulin, 'Lord of the Isles', is a roaring Atlantic gale, full of salt and smoke and seaweed.

The name comes from the Gaelic *Laggan Mhouillin*, 'The hollow where the mill is', and tradition says that in the 1740s this hollow was home to no less than ten illicit stills. There must have been something special about the place then, and clearly there still is. Surely, it is the combination of salt sea air and the richness of the Islay peat. I have been told that Lagavulin has twenty times as much exposure to peat reek as a typical Speyside whisky, and the water that runs down to the distillery is itself a soft peaty brown.

There is nothing hurried in the Western Isles and nothing hurried about Lagavulin. Long fermentation, long distillation and sixteen years in oak casks, breathing the salt sea air, make this the most powerful whisky of them all – dry, smoky, peaty, and with a taste of the sea. You will either love it or hate it; but if you love it, it will give you a wonderful experience, leading to a finish once described as a 'roaring crescendo'. If that doesn't make you want to try it, nothing will.

If you live in the Highlands, whether you be shepherd, fisherman or bank manager, there will be evenings when you come home and feel the need for instant warmth. Pour yourself a dram of 10 year old Talisker. It is the only malt whisky from '*Eilean a Cheo*', 'the Misty Isle', and although the distiller would probably shoot me for saying so, you might be forgiven for thinking that, to create this superb Island whisky, he mixed his malt with black pepper and a handful of gunpowder.

The distillery is at Carbost on the west coast of Skye, and Talisker has all the characteristics of an Island malt, though less pronounced than in the case of

Perhaps the Rev. Roderick Macleod had an influence on Talisker, after all.

Lagavulin – a deep amber colour and a smoky, seaweedy nose; but what sets it apart from all others is the initial fiery impact on the palate, followed by a long, long, peppery finish. It fills to perfection the huge gap between the Islay and the Speyside whiskies and provides a vastly superior alternative to central heating. Keep a bottle beside you and forget the storm outside.

Slainte Mhath!

Glossary of Scottish Words

(J) Refers to Jamieson's *Dictionary*

Bandsters	Binders
Ben	The inner apartment of a house (J)
Birse	Bristles
Bogle	Hide-and-Seek
Brae	Hill or slope
Brochan	Oatmeal boiled to a consistency somewhat thicker than gruel (J)
Brose	A kind of pottage made by pouring broth or water on meal (J)
Bughts	Sheepfolds
But	The outer apartment of a house (J)
Caird	Gypsy, pedlar
Carle	A person of low extraction (J)
Carlin	Old woman
Caterans	Bands of robbers, especially such as came down from the Highlands to the low country, and carried off cattle, corn, and whatever pleased them, from those who were not able to make resistance (J)
Ceithern	Fighting man (Gaelic)
Cogie	A small wooden barrel, or sometimes a wooden pail
Corby	Raven
Creich	Herd or group of animals
Cronach	Lament
Currach	Pannier or creel
Daffing	Joking
Fank	Sheep pens
Fleeching	Coaxing
Forhoo'd	Neglected
Garron	Highland pony
Gavel	End wall of a house – gable
Girdle	A circular plate of iron, for toasting cakes over the fire (J)
Goved	Stared, gazed
Gowans	Daisies

Greet	Weep, mourn
Grieve	Foreman, overseer
Hindberrye	Bramble
Houdie Craws	Hoody or Hooded Crows
Houf	Haunt
Ilk, Ilka	Each, every
Its lane	Alone, by itself
Joup	Mantle
Kelpie	The Spirit of the Waters, who, it was believed by the Northern nations, often assumed the form of a horse (J)
Leal	Loyal, faithful, true
Leglin	Milk pail
Leme	Glow, gleam
Loaning	Field or track
Loon	Rogue, worthless fellow
Low'd	Blazed, burned
Lum heid	Chimney stack
Lyart	Grey-haired
Mavis	Thrush
Melled	Mixed
Merk	A Scottish silver coin
Merle	Blackbird
Minny	Mother
Mooled	Literally 'Crumbled'. 'I wadna mool with him' – 'I would have no intimate fellowship with him' (J)
Mutches	Caps, head-dresses
Neeps	Turnips
Nolt	Cattle, oxen
Pleuch	Plough
Plewmell	Ploughing team
Roost	The inner roof of a cottage
Sark	Shirt
Sasine	Possession, from the old Scots 'sase', to seize or take hold of (J)
Shieling	A hut or residence for those who have the care of sheep. On the sides of the hills, upon spots where *shiels* have been occasionally erected to shelter the shepherds in summer, when feeding their flock at a distance from their ordinary dwellings, the sward is richly variegated with clover, daisies and other valuable grasses and wild flowers (J)

Skeelie	Skilful (J)
Skian dubh	Black knife (Gaelic)
Sowens	Flummery made from the dust of oatmeal remaining among the seeds, steeped and soured (J)
Speer	Enquire
Spulzie	Spoil, booty
Spunks	Matches
Swa'ed	Swelled
Tack	Lease of a house or farm
Tacksman	Leaseholder
Thole	Stand, withstand
Thrang	Through
Trig	Neat, trim
Uisge-beatha	Whisky (Gaelic – Water of life)
Unmeled	Unblemished
Waik	A row of deep damp grass
Weird	Fate, destiny. Weird sisters – The Fates (J)
Wene	Whin bush
Yorlin	Yellow-hammer

Further Reading

Rev. T.D. Miller	*Tales of a Highland Parish*
John Grant	*Legends of the Braes o' Mar*
W. M'Combie Smith	*The Romance of Poaching in the Highlands*
W. M'Combie Smith	*The Families of M'Combie and Thoms*
Alexander Mackenzie	*History of the Clan Mackenzie*
The Marchioness of Tullibardine	*A Military History of Perthshire*
Bishop Robert Forbes	*The Lyon in Mourning*
The Chevalier de Johnstone	*Memoirs of the Rebellion*
James Boswell	*Tour to the Hebrides with Dr Johnson*
John Jamieson	*Dictionary of the Scottish Language,* 1808